This book is due for return by the last date shown above.
To avoid paying fines please renew or return promptly.

Portsmouth
CITY COUNCIL
Library Service

CL-1

Trusted advice

Your **new baby**

A practical guide to your baby's first six months

DRmiriam**stoppard**

LONDON, NEW YORK, MUNICH,
MELBOURNE, AND DELHI

Author's dedication: For Josh

Revised Edition
Assistant Editor Dharini
Editor Bushra Ahmed
Designer Anchal Kaushal
Senior Designer Tannishtha Chakraborty
Managing Editor Suchismita Banerjee
Design Manager Arunesh Talapatra
DTP Operator Shanker Prasad
DTP Designers Pushpak Tyagi, Bimlesh Tiwary
DTP Manager Sunil Sharma
Picture Researcher Sakshi Saluja
Head of Publishing Operations Aparna Sharma

Project Editor Daniel Mills
Senior Art Editors Edward Kinsey, Isabel de Cordova
Managing Editor Penny Warren
Managing Art Editor Glenda Fisher
Publisher Peggy Vance
Senior Production Editor Jennifer Murray
Creative Technical Support Sonia Charbonnier
Senior Production Controller Man Fai Lau

First published by Dorling Kindersley in 1998
Reprinted 2001, 2006

This revised edition published in Great Britain in 2011
by Dorling Kindersley Limited
80 Strand, London WC2R 0RL
A Penguin Company

Copyright © 1998, 2001, 2006, 2011
Dorling Kindersley Limited
Text copyright © 1998, 2001, 2006, 2011
Dr Miriam Stoppard
The moral right of Miriam Stoppard to be identified
as the author of this book has been asserted.

The advice in this book is not intended as a substitute for
consultation with your healthcare provider. If you have any
concerns about the health of your baby, ask your doctor,
health visitor, or other health professional for advice.

Material in this publication was previously published
by Dorling Kindersley in Complete Baby and Childcare
by Dr Miriam Stoppard.

A CIP catalogue record for this book is available
from the British Library.

ISBN 978-1-4053-5652-7

Reproduced by Colourscan, Singapore
Printed in China by Leo Paper

Discover more at
www.dk.com

Contents

Chapter 1

Your newborn baby 9

Chapter 2

Holding and comforting 25

Chapter 3

Feeding 35

Chapter 4

Bathing, changing, and dressing 53

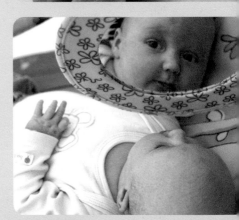

Chapter 5

Chapter 6

Introduction

Whether you're a mother expecting your first baby, have just given birth, or are an expectant or new father, you may be feeling apprehensive about your new role. Your delight at the prospect of having a baby may be mixed with anxiety about whether you'll be a good parent and can cope with bringing up a child. On top of this, you'll feel concerned for the happiness of your child if you mess things up. Don't worry: while parenting is one of the most responsible and challenging of all jobs, it's also one of the most rewarding.

The newborn baby

You've just experienced the creation of new life. Your baby is probably smaller than you imagined and he may seem very vulnerable. You may feel overwhelmed by joy, but you'll also be anxious to know whether your baby is all right, and whether the sounds and movements he makes are normal. Your doctor or midwife will do a few simple tests right after delivery, and the next day, to check that your baby is healthy. This will reassure you, and you'll probably be surprised at just how much your baby can do.

It's important for father and baby to bond, too. While mothers usually take most responsibility for a newborn's care, the father should be encouraged to take on an equal role. From the start, your baby's father should learn how to hold and care for your newborn. This way, your baby will very soon come to associate his father's specific smell and touch, and the sound of his voice, with comfort and reassurance.

Loving touch

All children benefit from close physical contact. You'll find that you instinctively hold your baby close, look into his eyes, and talk soothingly to him. He's more robust than you might think, and knowing this may help you to feel at ease when handling him. Feeding, bathing, and changing will go more smoothly if you hold him confidently.

All babies cry quite a lot – it's their only way of letting you know what they need. Within a few weeks, you'll learn to distinguish between the different cries that show your baby is hungry, niggling because he's bored, wants to be put down to sleep, or just wants a cuddle. Sometimes he'll cry for no obvious reason, but there are many remedies you can try to soothe and console him. Always be sensitive and alert to your baby's needs and respond to his cry. If you don't respond, he'll feel just as you would if you were ignored in a conversation.

Feeding and nutrition

Your newborn baby depends on you to meet all his nutritional needs. Feeding takes up a great deal of time, so it's essential to choose a method that suits you both. Breast milk is the perfect food. It contains all the nutrients in just the right amounts your baby needs. From your point of view, breastfeeding is also very convenient: there's no equipment to buy or sterilize, and no formula to make up.

If you don't want to breastfeed or choose not to, your baby can still thrive on a bottlefed diet, and one of the benefits of bottlefeeding is that your partner can be equally involved with feeding your baby. However, there is now extensive evidence regarding the health benefits of breastfeeding to baby and mother, as well as evidence to suggest that formula feeding may have associated health risks, such as increased chances of gastrointestinal infection.

Everyday care

Keeping your baby strong and healthy means not just giving him a good diet, but also looking after his physical comfort and hygiene each day. Many new parents worry about handling a very small baby in the baby bath, but you'll soon get used to bathtime and look forward to it as an opportunity to have fun and play with your baby. Instead of feeling anxious, set aside half an hour, have everything around you, and try to relax – you'll enjoy the experience.

Your newborn baby may need up to 10 nappy changes a day and you'll soon hardly believe there was once a time when you didn't know how to change a nappy! You can opt for disposable or fabric nappies, and will want to know the pros and cons of using either kind. Preventing nappy rash also means practising good nappy hygiene, and you can minimize the possibility of nappy rash if you follow a few commonsense guidelines.

With first clothes for your baby, look for cosy, comfortable garments in soft, natural fabrics that you can put on and take off him with the minimum of fuss. Dressing your baby will get easier with practice, so just be gentle and patient until you both get the hang of it.

Sleeping

Unless your newborn is hungry, cold, or uncomfortable in some other way, he'll spend most of the time between feeds asleep. It's important to consider what he'll sleep in and his sleeping environment, since research has shown that babies who get too hot are at a greater risk of cot death. Try to encourage your baby to sleep at night by tiring him out in the day with plenty of stimulation. If he frequently wakes you during the night, you'll find it difficult to cope.

Going out and about

Being organized and confident makes outings with your baby a great joy, and the sooner you start after bringing him home the better. When choosing equipment to carry or transport your baby, safety and portability should be your main considerations. It's worth spending time planning any trip so that you'll know where you can stop to change and feed your baby without inconvenience. For longer trips by car, preparation and attention to safety are paramount.

The rewards of parenting

A rule I've learned about parenting is that whatever you put in, you'll get back 500 times over. The sacrifices you make when your baby is very young will be replaced by more and more pleasures. One of the greatest rewards is to watch your baby develop and change from being a dependent and demanding person into a charming and thoughtful companion, an entertaining friend, and a good pal.

Chapter 1

Your newborn baby

You'll probably feel both **exhilarated** and exhausted when your baby is born. You may instantly feel **deeply attached** or bonding may take a little longer, but you'll soon start to see her **unique personality**.

The first moments

Whatever you had expected – bigger, smaller, quieter, less slippery – your baby will be a surprise and delight to you. Experienced parents discern a personality at birth but first-time parents may think their newborns are oblivious to the world about them. Babies, however, rapidly build up a vocabulary of sensory experiences right from the moment of birth. When awake, your baby will be alert and listening. She can respond when spoken to, recognize you by smell, and has an intent gaze. At birth she can recognize a human face, and she will move her head in response to noise. She is born wanting to talk and will "converse" with you if you talk animatedly, holding your head about 20–25 centimetres (8–10 inches) from her face; at this distance, she will be able to see you clearly. She will react to your smile in several ways: by moving her mouth, nodding, protruding her tongue, or jerking her whole body.

Handling your baby

The need for physical contact throughout childhood is well documented, and this is especially true of the first weeks of life. The majority of newborn babies spend much of their time asleep, so it is important that you're there to hold, mother, and respond to your baby when she's awake. If your baby is in an incubator, ask to be able to stroke her and change her nappy, at least. One young mother I met recently, whose 10-day-old baby had been in an incubator for the first 48 hours, was too terrified to pick him up because she thought he might "break". Babies are physically stronger than you might think, so don't worry too much.

Your baby's breathing

After an initial outburst of crying, you may not be able to hear anything more from your baby because it can be difficult to hear a newborn's light breathing. In some cases a baby may even stop breathing entirely for a few seconds, but this isn't abnormal or even cause for concern. All babies make strange noises when they breathe – usually a noisy, snuffling sound – and their breathing is often irregular.

Your baby's lungs are still weak, which means that her breathing is naturally much shallower and more rapid than yours or mine. This is nothing to worry about, as her lungs will gradually get stronger each day.

Suckling

For the first three days after your baby's birth, your breasts produce not milk but colostrum, which is a thin, yellow fluid that contains water, protein, sugar, vitamins, minerals, and antibodies that give, among other things, protection against infection.

To stimulate your breasts to produce milk, you need to feed her frequently; the sucking action of the baby stimulates hormones that, in turn, stimulate milk production. Even if you do not intend to breastfeed, it is a good idea to suckle your baby as soon as she is born, because the colostrum will be beneficial to her, and the act of suckling will help you bond with your baby.

As soon as your baby is born you can put her to your breast. Her natural sucking reflex and the sucking action will encourage the production of the hormone oxytocin. This hormone makes the uterus contract and expel the placenta. Touch your baby's cheek on the side nearest your nipple to stimulate her rooting reflex (see p. 38). Her lips should be on the breast tissue, with the whole of the nipple in her mouth.

Involving your partner

Because the experience of childbirth is so focused on the mother it is common for the father to feel neglected or excluded. It is important for father and baby to bond, too; touch, smell, and sound are good ways to do this. Soon after your baby is born, her father should hold her against his skin; this way she will come into contact with his specific smell, and over a period of weeks she will learn to associate this with comfort and reassurance.

The father should also speak to his child as she will quickly become familiar with his voice. In fact, if he talks to her while she is in the uterus, she will recognize her father's voice when she is born.

It is common for the mother to take prime responsibility for a newborn's care, but the father should be encouraged to take on an equal role. He should learn how to hold his baby and should build up a tactile relationship with her. Make sure he becomes involved with day-to-day routines such as bathing and nappy changing. Even if the baby is breastfed, he can learn to bottlefeed her by using expressed breastmilk from the mother. You and your partner should cuddle your baby when she and you are naked, so that she can feel and smell your skin and hear both your hearts beating.

Your baby's first breath

Don't be alarmed if your newborn cries vigorously – this is exactly the sound you want to hear.

Inside the uterus, your baby's lungs are redundant. She gets all the oxygen she needs from the placenta, so the lungs are temporarily collapsed.

The very first time your baby takes a breath, the lungs expand, and the increased pressure in them shuts a valve just beyond the heart, so that the blood that used to pass to the placenta for oxygenation now goes directly to the lungs. These two crucial actions make her an independent being, able to survive without you, and both actions happen in an instant.

Nothing should interfere with your baby's ability to take her first breath. That's why doctors and midwives clear air passages immediately and, if the first breath is delayed, they will resuscitate the baby.

Spots and rashes

Most newborns have harmless skin irritations, such as spots and rashes, in the first few days. They generally clear up within three weeks, by which time the skin has begun to stabilize.

Milia These small white spots are seen mainly on the bridge of the nose, but also elsewhere on the face. They're the result of a temporary blockage of the sebaceous glands, which secrete sebum to lubricate the skin. Never squeeze them: they will disappear of their own accord within a few days.

Heat rash If he's too warm, your baby may get small red spots, particularly on his face. Make sure that he isn't too warmly wrapped in clothing and blankets, and that you can regulate the temperature of his room (see p. 81).

Urticaria (hives) This is a kind of itchy rash in which the spots have a white centre and a red halo. It is quite common in the first week, and it may recur for a month or so. There is no need for treatment; it will disappear quite quickly.

How your baby looks

When you hold your baby for the first time, his appearance will probably surprise you. He's undoubtedly a joy to you, but you may have expected a clean and placid bundle, like the babies in advertisements for baby products. Real life (as you'll now suddenly discover) is a bit different.

First appearance

Skin A whitish, greasy substance – vernix – may cover your baby's skin. This natural barrier cream prevented the skin from becoming waterlogged in the uterus. It may be removed at once, or left to give your baby some natural protection against minor skin irritations such as flaking and peeling.

Blotchy skin is due to the tiny blood vessels being unstable. Black children are often light-skinned at birth, but the skin darkens as it begins to produce melanin, its natural pigment; it will reach its permanent colour by about six months.

Head Your baby's skull is made up of four large plates that haven't yet fused. This allows them to move across each other so that your baby can pass through the birth canal without hazard. His head may get slightly elongated or misshapen in the process; this is normal and doesn't affect the brain. Any swelling or bruising disappears in the first few days or weeks.

The soft spots on the top of your baby's skull where the bones are still not joined are called the fontanelles. In a sense, they are the windows into your baby's body. The skull bones won't fuse completely until he is about two. You may be able to see a faint pulse beating beneath his scalp.

Eyes Your baby may not be able to open his eyes straight away due to puffiness caused by pressure on his head during birth. This may also have broken some tiny blood vessels in his eyes, causing harmless small, red, triangular marks in the whites that need no treatment and disappear in a couple of weeks. He may have "sticky eye" – a yellow discharge around the eyelids. This is quite common, and although not serious should always be treated by a doctor.

Your baby may squint or look cross-eyed because although he can see clearly to a distance of 20 centimetres (8 inches) or so, he cannot focus both eyes at the same time beyond that. These conditions clear up as his eye muscles grow stronger (usually within a month); consult a doctor if he still squints at three months. If he is reluctant to open his eyes at first, never force them open. Most newborns have blue eyes. The colour is likely to change after birth, when a baby acquires melanin, the body's natural pigment.

Hair Some babies are born with a full head of hair, others are completely bald. The colour of your baby's hair at birth may not be the colour he will end up with later on. The fine downy hair that many babies have on their bodies at birth is called lanugo, and this will fall off soon after birth.

Genitals Many babies of both sexes appear to have enlarged genitals and "breasts" shortly after birth. This is due to the massive increase in hormone levels that you've experienced just before giving birth, some of which have passed into your baby's bloodstream. A baby boy may develop an enlarged scrotum and enlarged breasts, or even produce a little milk. This is not abnormal, and the swelling will gradually subside. A baby girl may have a swollen vulva or clitoris and a small "period" soon after birth.

Umbilicus The umbilical cord, which is moist and bluish-white at birth, is clamped with forceps and then cut with scissors. The remaining short length of cord will dry up and become almost black within two to four hours. The stump will shrivel up and fall off after about seven days, but your baby will feel no pain at all.

Umbilical hernia

Some babies develop a small swelling near the navel, called an umbilical hernia. This is caused when the abdominal muscles are weak, allowing the intestines to push through a little, which creates a bulge.

An umbilical hernia is most obvious when the abdominal muscles are used for crying. It is a very common occurrence, and virtually always clears up within a year. If your baby has one and it enlarges or persists, be sure to consult your doctor.

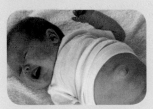

Site of swelling The hernia forms where the umbilical cord entered the baby's abdomen because there is a gap in the abdominal muscles at that point.

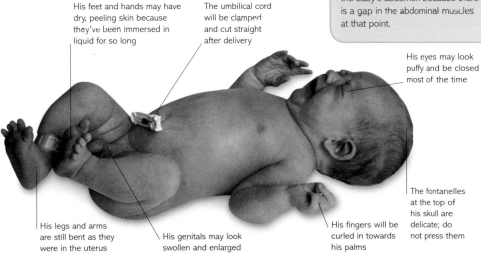

His feet and hands may have dry, peeling skin because they've been immersed in liquid for so long

The umbilical cord will be clamped and cut straight after delivery

His eyes may look puffy and be closed most of the time

His legs and arms are still bent as they were in the uterus

His genitals may look swollen and enlarged

His fingers will be curled in towards his palms

The fontanelles at the top of his skull are delicate; do not press them

About birthmarks

If you haven't found a single blemish anywhere on your baby's body, you probably haven't looked long enough.

Virtually every child is born with some kind of birthmark. Most will fade and disappear by the time your child is three, but some will remain and increase in size.

Both my sons had stork-bite birthmarks (see p. 15) at the back of the neck just under the hairline, a common place to find them. The marks disappeared within six months.

You might find a stork-bite mark anywhere, including on the neck, forehead, and eyelids.

Superficial birthmarks do no harm, are nothing to worry about, and need no treatment.

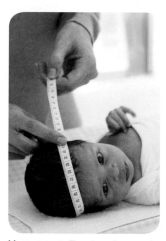

Measurements The circumference of your baby's head will be measured as well as his length. He will also be weighed.

Measurements

Your baby's weight, head circumference, and length will be measured shortly after birth to see how mature he is, and as a useful baseline for his development. Inevitably, they'll be compared to the "average", yet an average is just an arithmetical calculation: the "average child" doesn't exist.

Weight The range for babies born around their expected time is 2.5–4.5 kilograms (5½–10 pounds). If you're tall, heavy, or diabetic, your baby may be on the heavy side. Women with chronic hypertension, vascular or renal disease, or pre-eclampsia, or who smoke during pregnancy, are likely to have lighter babies. A baby born at less than 40 weeks is also likely to be lighter. Girls generally weigh slightly less than boys; twins or triplets weigh less than singletons.

It is common for your baby to lose weight in the first few days after birth as his body adjusts to new feeding requirements. He must now process his own food, and it will take a while for him to feed consistently. The usual weight loss at this time is about 115–170 grams (4–6 ounces). After a few days, you can expect your baby's weight to begin increasing.

A baby's weight gain tells us a great deal about his overall physical health. Steady weight gain indicates that his food intake is sufficient and that food is being absorbed; poor or erratic weight gain or weight loss signals that food intake is insufficient or that food isn't being properly absorbed.

Head circumference Your baby's head is disproportionately large to his body size; it is one-quarter of his length. The younger a baby is, the larger his head is in proportion to his body. The average circumference of a newborn baby's head is about 35 centimetres (14 inches). Measuring head circumference is regarded as a vital part of examining a baby because the growth of the head reflects the development of the brain; some experts think that there's a direct relationship between the circumference of the head and intelligence. An unusually large or small head circumference may indicate an abnormality in the brain.

Chest and abdomen The circumference of your baby's chest will be smaller than that of his head. His stomach might look very large, and even distended, but given the weakness of his abdominal muscles, this is to be expected.

The first nappies

Your baby's stools and urine may not look as you expect. If you have a baby girl, there may be some vaginal discharge. None of this necessarily means that something is wrong.

Stools Your baby's first bowel movement (which should be passed within the first 24 hours) consists of blackish-green meconium, which is mainly digested mucus. If he doesn't pass a motion during this period, inform your doctor or midwife, as he may have an obstruction.

It's not unusual for his next bowel movement to be two days later, especially if you are breastfeeding (check that your baby is wetting his nappy regularly, however). After the fourth day, he may pass four or five motions daily. You'll notice that the colour and composition of his stools change from the first blackish-green to greenish-brown, and then to a yellow semi-solid kind. If you are bottlefeeding your baby, the stools might resemble scrambled eggs.

Most babies fill their nappies as soon as they have eaten. This is due to a perfectly healthy reflex that makes the bowel empty itself as soon as food enters the stomach. Some babies pass motions much more infrequently, but as long as your baby does not have to strain and his motions are a normal colour and soft, there's no need for you to be concerned. If his motions are hard, you could offer more frequent breastfeeds – or, if he is formula fed, small amounts of cooled, boiled water between feeds.

Urine Newborns pass urine almost continuously because the bladder muscles are underdeveloped. Your baby may not be able to hold urine for any length of time (usually no longer than a few minutes), so it's normal to find that he wets his nappy up to 20 times in 24 hours. When he does, his urine will contain substances called urates that may stain his nappy dark pink or red. This, too, is quite normal for a newborn, but if you are anxious, consult your doctor or midwife.

Vaginal discharge Newborn girls sometimes produce a clear or white vaginal discharge. A small amount of vaginal bleeding can sometimes occur, but this is perfectly normal and will clear up naturally after a couple of days. If you are really worried, consult your doctor for reassurance.

Common birthmarks

Here are the most common types of birthmark your baby may have.

Salmon patches These reddish marks may be present at birth on the eyelids, nose, upper lip, and nape of the neck. No treatment is needed and most fade in infancy.

Strawberry marks These pink discolorations of the skin first appear as small red dots and usually fade within a few months. They may grow into red raised lumps, but these shrivel and disappear without leaving a scar.

Spider birthmarks (naevi) These marks appear shortly after birth as a network of dilated vessels. They generally disappear after the first year.

Pigmented naevi These brownish patches can occur anywhere on the body. They are usually pale and often enlarge as the child grows, but they seldom become darker.

Port wine stains These bright red or purple marks are caused by dilated capillaries in the skin.

Mongolian spots Dark bluish-black discolorations, usually on the buttocks or back, are often seen on dark-skinned babies. They fade naturally.

Stork bites These pink patches usually appear on the nose, neck, and eyelids. They may take about a year to disappear.

How your newborn behaves

Once your baby is born, it may take you a while to get used to his behaviour. It is worth taking the time to study his reactions to various stimuli, and becoming familiar with some of the traits that will mark his personality. Young babies have far more individuality than they are usually credited with, and this is a useful fact to bear in mind as you get to know your child.

Reflexes

One thing common to all healthy babies is a number of reflexes that can be stimulated from the very first moments after birth. These reflexes are unconscious movements that eventually – at about three months – start to be replaced by conscious movements.

Grasp reflex If you put something in the palm of your baby's hand, he will clench it surprisingly tightly. The grasp of a baby is often tight enough to support his entire body weight (although you should never try this).

Moro reflex When your baby's head is allowed to drop back, he will throw his limbs up with fingers and toes outstretched, then let them fall back slowly towards his body.

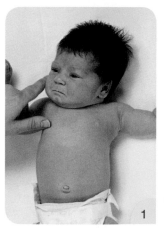

1 Rooting reflex This is your newborn's basic suckling reflex. Stroke his cheek gently with your finger.

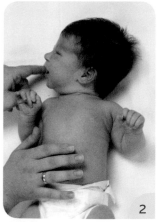

2 Suckling Your baby will turn his head at once in the direction of your finger and open his mouth to suckle.

You might notice that your newborn baby responds in a positive way to your presence by momentarily contracting the whole of his face and body. As he starts learning to control his movements, you will notice that his reactions become more directed and less random. For instance, at six weeks, instead of scrunching up his whole face, he may show you a distinct smile.

Testing reflexes Until your baby's physical and mental capabilities develop, it will be his instinctive reflexes that provide an indication of his maturity. Doctors can test these reflexes to check your baby's general health and see that his central nervous system is functioning properly. Premature babies will not react in the same way as full-term babies.

Although there are more than 70 primitive, unconscious reflexes that have been identified in newborn babies, your doctor is likely to test only a selected few. The two most commonly recognized reflexes that are easy to test yourself are the grasp and rooting reflexes (see p. 16). Don't attempt to test the Moro reflex (see p. 16) at home, because this could distress your baby and make him cry.

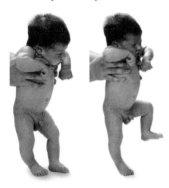

Walking reflex If you hold your baby under the shoulders so that he is in an upright position and his feet are allowed to touch a firm surface, he'll move his legs in a walking action. This reflex disappears in three to six weeks, and is not what helps your child learn to walk.

"Crawling" When you place your baby on his stomach, he will automatically assume what appears to be a crawling position, with his pelvis high and knees pulled up under his abdomen. When he kicks his legs, he may be able to shuffle in a vague "crawling" manner. It is not real crawling, however, and this behaviour will disappear as soon as his legs uncurl and he lies flat. There is good evidence that babies are born with the ability to find their own way to the breast following birth, much like puppies and kittens. If a baby is delivered onto mum's abdomen, he can often crawl his way up and attach himself to the nipple.

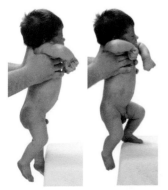

Stepping reflex This is quite similar to the walking reflex. If you hold your baby in an upright position and bring the front of his leg into contact with the edge of a table, he will lift his foot as if to step onto the table. The same reflex is in the arms: if the back of your baby's forearm touches the edge of the table, he will raise his arm as if to grasp it.

Your newborn girl

As soon as she is born, you can observe in your baby many behavioural traits that are typical of girls.

✴ Hearing in girls is very acute and they can be calmed down with soothing words much more readily than boys.

✴ If a baby girl hears another baby crying, she cries for longer than a boy would.

✴ Baby girls use their own voice to get their mother's attention earlier and more often than boys.

✴ Baby girls have no difficulty in locating a sound's source.

✴ Girls respond enthusiastically to visual stimulation right from the moment of birth.

✴ Baby girls are interested in everything that is unusual.

✴ Girls prefer the human face to almost anything else. Later in life, this trait shows as an intuitive ability to read facial expression, regardless of any cultural differences.

Coping with crying

Assume that your baby will cry a lot and it may be a pleasant surprise if she doesn't. If you think she won't cry and she does, you may find yourself overwhelmed and disoriented.

Remember that there are really only three states your newborn baby can be in: asleep, awake and quiet, or awake and crying. If she is crying, there are a variety of reasons for it. The most likely causes are tiredness, hunger, loneliness, and discomfort – she is too hot or too cold, in an uncomfortable position, or needs changing. You must accept sometimes, however, that a baby will cry for no apparent reason. This type of crying can be the most stressful for a parent.

Responding to crying Leaving a child to cry alone is never a good idea, even though you will hear this advice often. If a baby is denied attention and friendship in her early weeks and months, she may grow up to be withdrawn and shy. Research on newborns shows that if parents are slow to respond to their baby's crying, the result may be a baby that cries more rather than less. One study found that babies whose crying was ignored in their first weeks tended to cry more frequently and persistently as they grew older.

Often people confuse spoiling a child with loving a child. In my opinion a baby cannot be "spoiled" enough. A six-month-old baby who is picked up, nursed, cuddled, and talked to soothingly and lovingly is not learning about seeking attention; she is learning about love and forming human relationships – and that is one of the most important lessons a child will ever learn in terms of future emotional and psychological development. What we tend to call spoiling is both the natural response of a mother to a distressed child, and the natural need of her baby.

Sleep patterns and needs

Once you bring your baby home, you'll have some sleepless nights unless you are very lucky. Although most newborns usually sleep when they're not feeding, typically spending at least 60 per cent of their time asleep, some stay active and alert for surprisingly long periods during the day and night.

One young mother was shocked to find that her new baby never dozed for longer than one or two hours at a time until she was four months old. This is a very long time for any parent to last without a full night's sleep, especially when your body may be in need of rest after an exhausting pregnancy and birth. If your baby is very wakeful, take consolation in knowing that as long as she isn't left bored on her own, every minute of being awake she's learning something new – and in the long run you will be rewarded with an eager, bright child.

All babies are different, and their requirements for sleep depend on individual make-up. For this reason it makes no sense to lay down rigid sleeping times that correspond to the "average" baby; the average baby just doesn't exist.

Most newborns fall asleep soon after feeding. At first, a baby's wakefulness is likely to depend on how much feeding she needs, which in turn depends on her weight.

Sounds your baby makes

Whether asleep or awake, babies make a variety of strange noises, and this is quite normal. Most of them are due to the immaturity of the respiratory system and will soon disappear.

Snoring Your baby may make some grunting noises when she's asleep. This is not a true snore, and is probably caused by vibrations on the soft palate at the back of her mouth as she breathes in and out.

Snuffling Your baby may snuffle so loudly with each breath that you think she has a cold, or catarrh at the back of her throat. In most babies, these noises are harmless and are caused because the bridge of the nose is low, and air is trying to get through very short, narrow nasal passages. As your baby grows older, the bridge of her nose will get higher and the snuffling sound will gradually disappear.

Sneezing You may also think your baby has a cold because she sneezes a lot. In fact, sneezing is common in newborn babies, particularly if they open their eyes and are exposed to bright light. This sneezing can actually be beneficial – it helps clear out your baby's nasal passages.

Hiccups Newborn babies hiccup a lot, particularly after a feed. This leads some mothers to fear that their baby has indigestion, but this is rarely so. Hiccups are due to imperfect control of the diaphragm (the sheet of muscle that separates the chest from the abdomen) and they will disappear as your baby's control of the diaphragm matures.

Your newborn boy

From the moment of birth, baby boys show characteristic male behaviour, some of which will persist throughout life.

* Hearing in boys is less acute than in girls, so boys are more difficult to calm down.

* If a newborn boy hears another baby cry, he'll join in but stop crying quite quickly.

* Baby boys don't make sounds when they hear their mother's voice early on. This slow response lasts throughout life.

* Newborn boys find it difficult to locate the source of sounds.

* Baby boys need more visual stimulation than girls. They quickly lose interest in a design or picture, and lag behind girls in visual maturity up to the age of seven months.

* Baby boys are interested in the differences between things.

* Boys are more active, and are interested in things just as much as in people.

* Boys want to taste and touch everything, and move things about more than girls.

Checking her Apgar score

Immediately after birth, your baby will be given five short tests to assess her health. Each test is scored either 0, 1, or 2. A total of over 7 means she is in good condition. Under 4 means she needs help, and will receive resuscitation. Most low-scoring babies score highly when re-tested a few minutes later. The tests are:

Activity This shows the health and tone of your baby's muscles.

Pulse This indicates the rate and strength of her heartbeats.

Grimace/crying Facial expressions and responses show how alert she is to stimuli.

Appearance A pink skin colour shows that your baby's blood is properly oxygenated.

Respiration Breathing shows the health of her lungs.

Assessing a newborn The baby is checked to make sure that her lungs and heart are working properly and that her responses are healthy.

Keeping your newborn baby healthy

Whether you give birth in hospital or at home, the doctor or midwife will see that your baby gets expert uninterrupted attention until breathing is well established. Major problems should be identified within minutes so that any special care can begin as early as possible. Immediately after delivery, the doctor or midwife will test your baby against the Apgar scale (see left), and then examine her to assess her general condition. An experienced doctor or midwife can do these preliminary checks in less than a minute. You will then be able to rest easy, knowing that your baby is healthy and normal. The sort of checks your doctor will do involve:

✳ Making sure that she has normal facial features and that her body proportions are normal.
✳ Turning her over to see that her back is normal and that there is no spina bifida (a condition in which the coverings of the brain and spinal cord are left exposed).
✳ Examining her anus, legs, fingers, and toes.
✳ Recording the number of blood vessels in the umbilical cord.
✳ Weighing her and measuring her head and body length.
✳ Checking her temperature with a rectal thermometer and warming her if she needs it.

What happens the next day

Once all the initial tests have been carried out and you have suckled your baby, and you and your partner have held her for as long as you want, she will be wrapped up snugly and put in her cot to keep warm. She'll be given a thorough examination 24 hours later to ensure that all is well. This takes place when your baby is warm and relaxed. Ask the hospital staff to let you know when the doctor is going to perform the examination so that you can be there. This will give you the opportunity to discuss with your doctor any worries or questions that you may have at this stage.

Your baby will be placed on a flat surface, in a good light, and at a convenient height for the doctor, who may be seated. If you are immobile, you can have the examination at your bedside; if you cannot be there for some reason, always make sure to get the results. Your doctor will generally start examining at the top of the head and work down to the toes.

Head and neck The doctor will look at the skull bones and fontanelles (see p. 12) and check for any misshaping that occurred when the head passed through the birth canal. He will look at the eyes, ears, and nose; check the mouth for cleft palate, or any other abnormality, and teeth (they are rare but not unknown); and check the neck for cysts or swellings.

Chest and heart The heart and lungs are checked with a stethoscope. The lungs should be expanded and working normally. After birth, the workload of a baby's heart increases when she becomes responsible for her own circulation. This may cause a heart murmur, but most murmurs soon disappear. Your child will be examined during the postnatal checkup to see if a heart murmur persists.

Arms and hands The doctor will check each arm for a pulse, and for normal movement and strength. He will also check the fingers and palm creases. Nearly all babies have two major creases across each palm; if there is only one, your doctor will look for other physical abnormalities.

Abdomen and genitals The doctor will gently press your baby's abdomen to check the size and shape of the liver and spleen (in newborns, both may be slightly enlarged). He will check a boy's testes to ensure that they are properly descended and a girl's labia to see that they are not joined and that the clitoris is a normal size. He will also check the lower spine and anus for congenital abnormalities.

Hips, legs, and feet The doctor will hold both thighs firmly and move each leg to see if the head of the thigh bone is stable, to test for congenital dislocation of the hip. (This is not painful, but the movement may make your baby cry.) He will examine her legs and feet to make sure they are of equal size. If the ankle is still turned inwards as it was in the uterus, your baby may have a club foot. This can be treated with manipulation and perhaps a cast.

Nerves and muscles The doctor will manipulate your baby's arms and legs to make sure they are not too stiff or floppy, and to check the health of her nerves and muscles. He will make sure that normal newborn reflexes are present (see pp. 16–17), and check your baby's head control.

If your baby has jaundice

This is not a disease and, in the majority of newborn babies, is not dangerous.

Jaundice is likely to occur when a baby is about three days old. It is caused by the breakdown of red blood cells shortly after birth. This breakdown creates an excess in the blood of a pigment called bilirubin, causing a yellowish tinge to the baby's skin.

A newborn is unable to excrete the bilirubin sufficiently rapidly to prevent jaundice until her liver is more mature, at about one week.

In most babies jaundice doesn't require treatment and clears up by itself within a week. The level of bilirubin can be checked with a blood test. Some babies do need treatment, usually with phototherapy – exposure to ultraviolet light for about 12 hours.

Rhesus compatibility (incompatibility between the blood types of mother and baby, usually a Rhesus-negative mother with a Rhesus-positive baby) is now a rare cause of severe jaundice in newborn babies as it is usually diagnosed and treated antenatally. Other less common causes of jaundice are hepatitis and biliary atresia, a rare condition in which the bile duct fails to develop properly.

Looking after your new baby

During the last weeks of pregnancy, it's a good idea for you and your partner to spend time discussing and planning how you are going to run your domestic routine once you settle down at home with your new child. If your partner is both willing and able to play a full part (or if he can be encouraged to do so), you should be able to cope without too much difficulty; if not, you should get someone in to help you, especially for the first few weeks.

The first few days of motherhood will be harder than you think. Labour and birth are physically and emotionally draining; you'll feel you have very few reserves, and you will also be extremely fatigued. You will realize, once you are at home with your baby, that one job or activity succeeds another almost without respite, and in the middle of all this action you are still learning about being a mother. Even if you have read every baby book going, you will find that your baby conforms to no typical schedule or plan, and that you have to work out your life around your baby's routine. It is a mistake to try to impose a routine on your baby, and will only cause you more work; you have to take your lead from her. As far as your sleep is concerned, get it when you can: new babies don't know night from day and need the same attention during the night as during the day.

In the first few weeks at home with your baby, try to get someone else to be responsible for all the household chores, or simply cut back the amount of work that you do to the bare

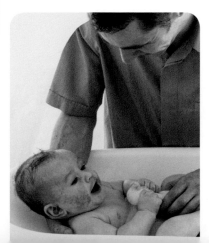

Sharing the baby's care
Taking over responsibilities, such as bathing the baby, can be a joyful experience for a new dad, forming a strong bond between father and child.

minimum, until you become used to the schedule that your baby follows naturally. Remember that you can only do your best and that it's important to look after yourself and your own health, too.

Sources of help

Unless you want to risk becoming extremely tired, even depressed and weepy, you will need some help to tide you over at least the first few days with your baby, and preferably the first week or two. Don't be too proud to ask for or accept help in household tasks or babycare; if you are too reticent, you may soon come to regret it. Having someone help out does not mean that you are in any way inadequate as a mother. The best possible solution is some live-in help, so that your day can be split into shifts. That way, you can at least make sure that you get sufficient rest and pay attention to your diet.

Family and friends Your mother and your mother-in-law are probably the people you can trust most in the world when it comes to childcare. They have had children of their own and are experienced at looking after babies, which means they are the ideal people to give you lots of helpful support and advice. A good idea would be to ask one of them (or a sister, other relative, or friend) to come and live in your house around the time you expect to go into labour. That way, she can become familiar with the routine you have established in your home with your family and partner, and be ready to receive and help you when you come home with the baby.

Such a helper is invaluable. You will feel confident that your household is ticking over quite normally. She should take off your shoulders all the administration and see to meals, laundry, shopping, and so on. This can relieve some of the responsibility from your partner, so you will both be able to devote more time to your baby. In addition, if your helper has had children of her own, she can be a source of information and welcome advice.

Nannies If you decide that you would like a nanny, try to arrange for her to be settled in with your family before the baby is born. This is a very good idea because it gives you time to get to know each other. You will develop a sense of rapport (or not, as the case may be) and you should be able to tell whether or not you are going to get on together. Having a newborn baby in the house is quite demanding and

Maternity nurses

If you want short-term, live-in help, consider hiring a maternity nurse. She will join your household just before or after the baby is born and will help you with all of the babycare.

As well as providing welcome help with the baby, maternity nurses are invaluable teachers. They will show you how to take care of your baby's daily needs: how to change nappies, how to breast- or bottlefeed her, how to know when your baby's had enough, and how to take the baby carefully off your breast to avoid soreness and cracked nipples, for example.

But it's up to you and the nurse to work out the regime you would like. You may decide, for instance, that you wish to have an uninterrupted night's sleep; the nurse will be on duty through the night but you will take over at, say, 7 a.m. so that she can get some rest. Later on in the day, she would be responsible for the baby's laundry, preparation of formula feeds, keeping the nursery clean, and looking after all the baby's needs and some of yours, too.

A maternity nurse usually does not stay in a home for more than four weeks – but you can arrange for her to stay for longer if your finances permit. Maternity nurses are expensive, but hiring one will get you off to a good start if there is no-one else to help.

exhausting, and it is important to have a helper who will fit in with your routines and adapt to your lifestyle. You must also have confidence in her abilities and feel happy with her relationship with your baby.

By far the best way to find a nanny is through the personal recommendation of a trusted friend. Another way is through a reliable nanny agency. Not all of them are dependable, but the Recruitment and Employment Confederation (see p. 93) can advise you on finding the most reliable one in your area. Very high-class nanny agencies are not necessarily the best, and you will pay more for your nanny from one of these than from other agencies. Internet nanny agencies can be a cheap and convenient alternative, and websites such as www.netmums.com and nanny sharing forums allow you to get personal recommendations from other mums.

Advertising for a nanny is another option. But no matter how you recruit your nanny, it is absolutely essential that you see her at least twice before you hire her. On the first occasion you could have a formal interview, and on the second you could relax over some lunch or tea or maybe go shopping together. By doing this you will learn more about her, get a clearer picture of her personality, and be able to judge whether you will actually get on together.

Draw up some kind of employment contract in which you cover the important aspects of the job, including the required approaches and attitudes. Make certain any tasks are carefully and clearly laid out; make it plain that instant dismissal may follow if your instructions are not followed. Your nanny should be prepared to bend her usual practices in order to adapt to and fit in with yours, but it would be pointless hiring someone who is a strict disciplinarian if you want your children to be brought up in a liberal and laid-back manner. Only you know, however, exactly how you want your baby treated, so you must discuss each and every one of your relevant likes and dislikes (however trivial they may seem) with your prospective nanny.

Au pairs These young women (or sometimes young men) from abroad will help you with your baby in exchange for room, board, and a small wage. An au pair is cheaper than a nanny, but bear in mind that most will probably have no training in childcare, and may speak little English. An au pair is supposed to live with you as part of the family; she is not an employee. It's not a good idea (and not fair on your au pair) to leave her in sole charge of a baby under one year of age for any length of time.

Chapter 2

Holding and comforting

You may be anxious picking up your newborn, in case you somehow damage him. In fact, children benefit from physical contact, and you can be confident that holding him is good for both of you.

Putting your baby down

Make sure you always lay your baby on his back.

Research has demonstrated that babies who sleep on their stomachs are at greater risk of cot death than babies who sleep on their backs. Publicity in the UK about this finding has resulted in a significant drop in cot deaths.

Handling and carrying

A newborn baby may appear very vulnerable and fragile, but he is more robust than you might think. With this knowledge, you will be able to inspire confidence rather than uncertainty in your child. For the baby's comfort, and for your own peace of mind, you must feel at ease when you handle him. You must also be able to hold your baby confidently in order to bathe, dress, and feed him successfully.

Handling your baby

When you move your baby, your action must be as slow, gentle, and quiet as possible. You'll find that you instinctively hold your baby close, look into his eyes, and talk soothingly to him. Not surprisingly, it has been proven that all children benefit from close physical contact, particularly when they can hear the familiar sound of your heartbeat. For example, premature babies gain more weight when they lie on fleecy sheets, which give them the sensation of being touched. The best way to ensure skin contact with your child is for both of you to lie naked in bed. Here he can smell and feel your skin, and hear your heartbeat. In this way, too, you can make sure that he

How to pick up your baby

1 Lift your baby Slide one hand under your baby's neck and the other hand under his back and bottom to support his lower body securely.

2 Support his head Pick him up gently and smoothly. Always be sure to support your baby's head with your hand so that it doesn't flop back.

3 Cradle him in your arms Transfer your baby to a carrying position. He will feel safe and secure cradled in the crook of your elbow.

becomes familiar with the smell of his father's skin. Skin-to-skin contact or "kangaroo care" has been known to help preterm infants develop and grow healthier. It helps establish breastfeeding by encouraging your baby to latch on to the breast instinctively.

Make sure to support your baby's head whenever you pick him up and put him down: he has little control over it until he's about four weeks old. If his head flops back, he'll feel that he's going to fall, his body will jerk, and he'll stretch out his arms and legs in the Moro, or "startle", reflex (see p.16).

Pick up and put down your baby with your whole arm supporting his spine, neck, and head. Swaddle your baby tightly to make him feel secure; it's a useful way to comfort a distressed baby. Wrap him firmly in a shawl or blanket so that his head is supported and his arms are close against his body. Once you lay him in the cot, unwrap him gently.

Two ways to carry your baby

Carry your baby in your arms by cradling his head in the crook of one slightly inclined arm. The rest of his body will rest on the lower part of your arm, encircled by your wrist and hand, which support his back and bottom. Your other arm provides additional support to his bottom and legs, and your baby can see your face as you talk to and smile at him.

Alternatively, hold your baby against your upper chest with his head on your shoulder. Place your forearm across his back, with your hand supporting his head. Use your other hand to support your baby's bottom, or to help yourself balance.

Cradling your baby Hold your baby's head and support the length of his body when carrying him. Holding your baby close will make him feel safe, especially if he can see your face.

Carrying your baby in a sling

Newborns are best carried in lightweight slings worn on the chest, where they feel secure and close to you.

* Choose a sling made from a washable fabric, since it will get dirty as you carry your baby.

* The sling must be easy to put on and comfortable to wear for both you and your partner. Try it out with your baby before you decide to buy it.

* The sling should ensure good support to your baby's head and neck, and keep him secure. He must not be able to slip out of the sides of the sling.

* The shoulder straps must be wide enough to support your growing baby's weight. Wide shoulder straps will also make carrying more comfortable.

* It has been said that a baby shouldn't be carried in a sling until he can support his own head. This is not true. A sling can be used as soon as you and your baby are comfortable with it.

* Some slings are specifically designed so that you can breastfeed your baby while he is in the sling.

Benefits for parents

Massage is a delightful and valuable activity that has advantages for you and your partner, too.

✳ Massaging your newborn baby helps to enhance the bonding process between you and your child.

✳ If you are anxious or have had little experience with children, massage allows you to get used to handling your new baby with confidence.

✳ Playing music or singing softly to your baby during massage can also help to calm your nerves with its relaxing effects.

✳ You'll find that massaging your baby's soft, smooth skin is a comforting experience for both of you.

Baby massage

Massage can have all the benefits for a baby that it has for an adult; it can calm a fretful baby, and is a marvellous way of showing love. If you massage your baby every day, he will learn to recognize the routine and will show pleasure as you begin. You can continue to massage your baby as he gets older; a massage is often the ideal way to calm and soothe an excited toddler.

Provide a relaxed atmosphere before you start. Since this will be a new experience for you both, any distractions can spoil the mood and upset your baby. Choose a time when there is no-one else around and turn off the phone. Make sure the room is comfortably warm. Lay your baby on a warm towel or sheepskin, or on your lap. Work from his head down, using light, even strokes, and ensure that both sides of his body are massaged symmetrically. Make eye contact with your baby throughout the massage and talk quietly, gently, and lovingly to him.

Giving a massage

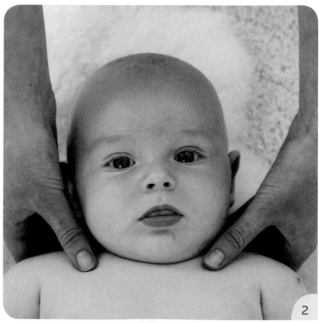

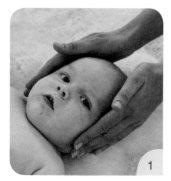

1 **Head and face** Lightly massage the crown of your baby's head in a circular motion, then stroke down the sides of his face. Massage his forehead, working from the centre out; move over his eyebrows and cheeks and finish around his ears.

2 **Neck and shoulders** Gently massage your baby's neck from his ears down to his shoulders, and from his chin to his chest. Then stroke his shoulders from his neck outwards.

3 Arms and hands
Stroke down his arms right to his fingertips. Using your fingers and thumb, gently squeeze all along each arm, starting at the shoulder.

Benefits for your baby

Your baby can only gain from the pleasures and sensations he feels when you give him a loving massage.

* Your baby loves being with you and the intimate contact of massage enhances this feeling. He will recognize it as a definite sign of your love.

* If your baby is unsettled, he will be calmed by the soothing strokes of your hands. This will make him feel secure and relieve his anxiety.

* A massage can often ease minor digestive upsets, for instance wind, which may be making your baby fretful.

* Babies need touch; research has shown that babies would rather be stroked than fed.

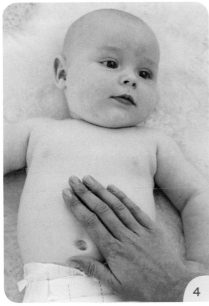

4 Chest and abdomen Gently stroke down your baby's chest, following the delicate curves of his ribs with your fingers. Rub his abdomen in a circular motion and work slowly in a clockwise direction from the navel outwards. (Make sure to go gently over his navel and abdomen.)

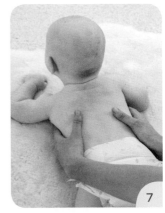

5 Legs and ankles Now you can massage your baby's legs, working from his thighs down to his knees. Stroke down the shins, and move around to his calves and ankles. Gently squeeze all the way down.

6 Feet and toes
Massage your baby's ankles and feet, stroking from heel to toe, and then concentrate on each toe individually. Finish massaging his front with some long, light strokes up and down the whole length of his body.

7 Massaging your baby's back Once you have finished massaging your baby on the front, turn him over and work gently on his back.

Girl and boy babies differ in why and how much they cry, and in how they respond to attempts to soothe them.

✳ Baby girls are less vulnerable to stress at the time of birth than boys, and less likely to cry.

✳ Girls are less likely than boys to cry in new situations; boys tend to take longer to adapt.

✳ Mothers tend to give extra attention to girls who cry a lot.

✳ Boys cry more readily than girls if parental attention and love are not forthcoming.

✳ Boys are less likely to get extra attention when they cry a lot: their mothers mistakenly want them to be tough.

Crying and comforting

All babies cry quite a lot and yours will too, so be prepared for it. There will be times when the reason for his crying is obvious and easily remedied: he's hungry, too hot, too cold, bored, uncomfortable because of a wet or a dirty nappy, or he might simply want your closeness and affection. One reason for crying that parents often fail to recognize is the desire for sleep. I well remember trying to console my newborn son in all kinds of ways before it occurred to me that he just wanted to be left alone to sleep.

Very young babies cry when they are disturbed, when roughly handled, for instance at bathtime, or when they get a shock – perhaps from feeling that they are going to be dropped, from a loud noise, or from a bright light. A two-week-old baby always responds to the security of being firmly wrapped in a shawl or held in strong, confident arms. Once you have investigated your baby's crying, don't worry too much about it – crying is practically his only way of communicating his needs to you. Interestingly, it is now known that breastfed babies communicate very effectively, using body language long before they cry. They do this by, for example, snuffling, licking their lips, and salivating quite obviously, and a mum who is breastfeeding her baby will recognize these cues long before he starts to cry. A mum who says that her baby never really cries may simply be very tuned to his needs.

Recognizing different cries Within a few weeks, you can distinguish between the different cries that mean your baby is hungry, is niggling because he is bored, wants to be put down to sleep, or just wants a cuddle. Your baby is learning about you and how to communicate with you, too. He cries out of need and you respond by giving him what he wants.

Responding to your baby

I believe you should respond quite quickly to your baby's cry. If you don't respond, then your baby feels just as you would if you were being ignored in a conversation. There is a considerable amount of research to show that your baby is affected by how you respond when he is crying. For instance, mothers who respond quickly to crying are likely to have children with greater and more advanced communication skills, including speaking and outgoing behaviour. Babies who are ignored cry more often and for longer in the first year than

Good communication The only way your baby can make his needs known is by crying, so always respond.

babies who are attended to quickly. It seems that mothers cause their babies to settle into a pattern of crying often and persistently because they fail to respond, and a vicious circle is set up in which the baby cries, the mother fails to respond, the baby cries more, and the mother is even less inclined to act. A sensitive response promotes self-confidence and self-esteem in your child's later life. Some mothers believe that always responding will "spoil" their babies. A young baby has a limitless capacity for soaking up love: there's no way that you can spoil a baby by attention in his first year.

Crying spells

Most babies have crying spells. Often crying occurs in the late afternoon or early evening, when your baby may cry for as long as half an hour. If your baby has colic (see p. 33), evening crying spells can last up to two hours. At one time mothers used to say that a child required this exercise to help develop healthy lungs and therefore felt they could leave their babies to cry. This is nonsense; you should always try to console your baby during a crying spell.

Once your child establishes a pattern of crying spells, it may go on for several weeks. It's understandable – it's your baby's way of becoming adjusted to being in a very different world from that experienced inside your uterus. The more sensitively you respond to him and take your lead from him, the more rapidly he will become acclimatized to his new life; the sooner you accommodate his likes and dislikes, the sooner crying spells will stop.

Night-time crying

There is no doubt that every parent finds crying spells hard to cope with, especially at night. Don't get frustrated because your child doesn't respond to your attempts to soothe him. If walking up and down, singing songs, or swaddling just don't seem to work, you could take him for a short drive; the gentle swaying motion of a car may send him to sleep.

During the night, crying will make you feel impatient at the least, and at the worst, that you will do anything to stop your baby crying. These feelings are quite normal, so don't become frightened and tense – otherwise the crying will just get worse. When my five-day-old baby cried persistently during the night, I actually thought that if I threw him against the wall he would stop. I didn't, of course, but it is quite normal to think such things; it would have been abnormal only if I had done it.

If your baby cries a lot

There's research that shows that your child may cry despite your best efforts to console him, regardless of whether or not he feels any discomfort.

* Babies of mothers who have had a general anaesthetic during labour, and babies who have been delivered by forceps, tend to cry more in the first weeks of life.

* Babies born after a long labour are likely to sleep in short bursts, and to cry quite a lot between naps.

* If you are tense, irritable, and impatient, you will undoubtedly communicate your mood to your baby, who will sense it and cry.

* There are also individual and racial differences between babies. Some cry a different amount even if they're given the same care and attention.

* Some parents find cranial osteopathy helpful to manage their crying baby. I am not sure how accepted this is from a medical point of view, but it is certainly not harmful.

Are dummies safe to use?

Babies are born with a sucking reflex. Without it, they wouldn't suckle or be able to nourish themselves. I feel it's important that babies are allowed to indulge their desire to suck.

Some babies are more "sucky" than others; I certainly had one who wanted to suck all the time, whether he was hungry or not. With all four of my sons, I used to put their thumb gently into their mouth so they could suck to soothe themselves.

Current research suggests that routine dummy use can undermine breastfeeding. Dummy use has also been linked with increased risk of ear infections. Speech and language therapists too are often concerned that dummy use can inhibit language development. There are also dental health concerns associated with long-term dummy use. However, there has been some research to suggest a reduced risk of cot death if a baby uses a dummy while sleeping. So it's really up to you to decide what's best for your baby.

Soothing your baby

If feeding and changing don't seem to settle your baby, there are other ways you can try to console him. Most babies respond to either movement or sound, or both. So taking them out in the car will be effective because of the motion of the vehicle and the steady humming sound of the engine. If your baby seems fretful even after your best efforts to soothe him, try some (or all) of the following remedies as part of your repertoire of crying cures (you may find that these movements and sounds relax you as well, which in turn will benefit you both):

✳ Any movement that rocks him, whether it is you holding and rocking him in your arms, going gently back and forth on a swing, or rocking him in a cradle or rocking chair.

✳ Walking or dancing with an emphasis on rhythmic movement, since it will remind him of the time when he was being jogged inside your uterus.

✳ Bouncing him gently in your arms, the cot, or on the bed.

✳ Putting him in a sling (see p. 27) and walking around with him. If you're on your own, just get on with whatever you want to do and try to ignore the crying.

✳ Taking him for a ride in the car or in a pram, or for a walk in a sling, even at night (you may want to take a phone with you).

✳ Any form of music as long as it is calm, rhythmic, and not too loud; nowadays specially recorded sleeping mp3s and CDs are available.

✳ A noisy toy that your baby can shake or rattle.

✳ A steady household noise, for instance, the humming of the washing machine.

✳ Your own soft singing voice can be soothing, especially if you sing a lullaby.

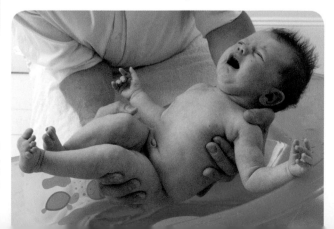

Bathtime crying Many young babies cry when they are having a bath, simply because they hate having their skin exposed to the air.

What to do when your baby cries

CAUSE OF CRYING	WHAT TO DO
Hunger A hungry cry is nearly always the first cry a parent recognizes and it is the most common reason that young babies cry. They rarely cry after feeding. Babies love the sensation of a full stomach.	Feed on demand. If you have a baby who wants to suck all the time, you don't need to feed; just give him a drink of cooled, boiled water in a sterile feeding bottle.
Tiredness Until they're used to their new world, babies cry when they are tired. An observant parent realizes this and will put the baby down.	Lay your baby down where he is quiet and warm. It will also help to wrap or swaddle him before you put him down to sleep.
Lack of contact Some babies will stop crying as soon as you pick them up, because all they want is comfort and a cuddle.	Pick up your baby as soon as he cries. Carry him in a shawl or a sling. Lay him tummy-down across your lap and massage his back.
Startling A jerky movement, sudden noise, bright light, or rough physical games can upset your baby.	Hold your baby close, rock him gently, and sing to him. Avoid anything that will startle him.
Undressing Most babies dislike undressing; it puts them through unfamiliar movements and they hate the feel of air on their skin.	Undress your baby as little as possible in the first few weeks. When you do, keep up a running commentary of reassuring talk.
Temperature Babies tend to cry if they become too hot or too cold. They may cry if a wet or soiled nappy gets cold or if they are suffering from nappy rash.	Keep your baby's room at 16–20°C (61–68°F). Take off blankets and clothing if he's too hot; add a blanket and another layer of clothing if he's too cold. Change his nappy if necessary.
Pain A ear infection, colic (see right) or other sources of pain may cause your baby to cry. If his ear hurts, he may hit it with his fist.	Cuddle your baby and talk soothingly to him. Remove any obvious source of pain, such as an uncomfortable nappy fastening. If he seems ill, seek medical advice.

Coping with colic

Colic is the name for bouts of unexplained crying. These are usually in the late afternoon or evening but can be at any time. The baby's face becomes red, the legs are drawn up to the abdomen, and the fists clenched.

Colic generally stops by the age of three to four months, is rarely serious, and needs no treatment. However, parents find it very distressing. It is not known why it happens but it usually starts in the first three weeks of a baby's life. It is well recognized that colicky babies are quite healthy and continue to thrive.

All sorts of causes have been put forward, such as overfeeding, underfeeding, wind in the bowel, being picked up too much or too little, indigestion, and tension. Usually, tension is the most likely cause. You're preoccupied in the evening with bedtime for the baby and getting your evening meal. It is likely that your baby picks up on the tension, and normal that he should respond with a crying spell.

I'm against using any kind of medicine for colic. Of course you should try to soothe your baby but don't expect him to respond readily. Take comfort from the fact that these spells last for only three months, so there is light at the end of the tunnel.

Don't be afraid to ask for support if you find it hard to cope with the stress.

Be sensitive to your baby's needs

You have to learn to read your baby's signals and gain insight into his needs and desires. Not being able to read these signals, whether they be "I'm hungry", "I'm tired", or "I want to be cuddled, not played with", can all result in tears. Once you recognize your baby's cry you have to respond to it, otherwise he's bound to scream even louder and longer. Prolonged crying may make your baby feel very tired, even exhausted, and he will become extremely irritable and difficult to soothe. More importantly, he will quickly learn that pleas for attention go unheeded, and that there's no loving human response when he needs it.

Always be sensitive and alert to your baby's needs. Look, listen, and do your best to interpret what he is trying to say to you through his behaviour; then resolve whatever is causing the alarm immediately. There are all sorts of signs of small discomforts to which you must attend. When your baby has a cold, for instance, his nose may get blocked, making it impossible for him to breathe and eat at the same time, so he'll become angry and frustrated and almost certainly cry.

As you and your baby get to know each other, you will learn to understand what he really wants. If you know, for example, that he's hungry, don't delay his feed by deciding to give him a bath first, simply in order to stick to your routine. Occasionally, you have to ignore routines so that you can respond to your baby's crying.

Chapter 3

Feeding

Infant feeding is about **providing adequate nutrition** for your baby. The main things you need to remember are that you should **take the lead from your baby**, and that the **love and affection** you give to her are as important as any milk.

Milk: the perfect food

In the first few months, your baby will get all the nutrients she requires from breast or formula milk. These contain:

Calories The energy content of food is measured in calories. Infants require around two-and-a-half to three times more calories than adults for their body weight.

Carbohydrates These are the principal source of calories.

Protein This is essential for building body tissues. A baby's protein requirement is three times as great as an adult's on the basis of body weight.

Fats Minute traces of fatty acids are needed for the baby's growth and cell repair.

Breastfeeding Suckling helps to form a very strong bond between you and your baby from the start.

What your newborn baby really needs

Your baby depends on you for adequate nutrition: breast or bottled milk provides all a newborn needs. But although breast milk is her perfect food, your baby will thrive even if you choose to bottlefeed. Feeding takes a great deal of time, so it's essential to choose a method that suits you both.

A baby's nutritional needs reflect her rapid growth in the first months of life: most babies double their birthweight in around four to five months. For healthy development, your baby's food must contain adequate amounts of calories, carbohydrates, protein, fats, vitamins, and minerals (see left and p. 37), and until she's at least six months old, your baby will receive all these nutrients from breast or formula milk. Your baby will tell you when she is hungry, so take your lead from her in setting the pattern of feeds.

Why breast is best

Human breast milk is the perfect food for babies. Because it doesn't look as rich and creamy as cow's milk, you may think it's not good enough for your baby, but don't be put off. It contains all the nutrients in just the right amounts she needs and has many benefits for her. Breastfed babies tend to suffer less than bottlefed babies from illnesses such as chest infections because antibodies from the colostrum (see p. 38) and the breast milk protect the baby and keep her healthy. These antibodies also protect the intestine, reducing the chances of diarrhoea and vomiting.

Breastfed babies don't get constipated, since breast milk is more easily digested than cow's milk. However, they pass few stools because the milk is so completely digested that there is little waste. They are also less prone to nappy rash (see p. 67). From your point of view, breastfeeding is very convenient: you don't need to warm up the milk, there are no bottles to sterilize, no formula has to be made up, and there's no equipment to buy. Breastfed babies usually sleep longer than bottlefed babies, suffer less from wind, and posset (regurgitate milk) less.

Don't worry if your baby seems chubbier than other babies of her age. Each baby has its own appetite and metabolic rate, and your baby will be the right weight for her own body.

Breastfeeding can help you regain your figure more quickly. Your breasts may change in size or sag after the birth, but this comes from being pregnant not from breastfeeding, which helps you lose weight gained in pregnancy. While you are breastfeeding, the hormone oxytocin (see p. 38), which stimulates milk flow, encourages the uterus to return to its pre-pregnant state; your pelvis and waistline will get back to normal more quickly, too. Additionally, breastfeeding provides significant protection against breast cancer and ovarian cancer and also reduces the risk of developing osteoporosis in later life.

Bottlefeeding

Every woman is capable of breastfeeding her baby, and you should try to do so. Many women think they must breastfeed to be good mothers, and feel guilty if they decide not to. On the other hand, some women find it emotionally or psychologically difficult to breastfeed; others realize that they simply cannot master breastfeeding. If, after seeking support, you choose to discontinue breastfeeding and concentrate on giving your baby a bottlefed diet, she will still thrive.

You may consider bottlefeeding if you feel that breastfeeding will tie you down, particularly if you intend to return to work very soon after the birth. This may be the best solution for you, but remember that it is possible to express enough milk so that your partner or a childminder can feed your baby while you are away from home. That way, your baby can have all the benefits of your milk, and you can have the flexibility and freedom of bottlefeeding.

A feature of bottlefeeding is that your partner can be as involved with feeding your new baby as you are. He should start as soon as possible after the birth, so that he can learn to handle your baby confidently and understand her needs.

Feeding It is really important to make feeding a time of security and closeness for you and your baby.

Vitamin and mineral needs

As well as the basic nutrients (see p. 36), milk will supply your baby with necessary vitamins and minerals.

Vitamins: These are essential for health. Newborn babies cannot make vitamin K, so your baby will be given a vitamin K injection soon after birth. After the age of six months, if your baby is drinking less than 500ml (1 pint) of formula milk every day, she may need supplementary vitamin drops. However, do not give her more than one supplement as too much of a vitamin can be harmful; do not, for example, give her both vitamin drops and cod-liver oil. Consult your health visitor if you need advice.

Minerals: Breast and formula milk contain magnesium, calcium, and phosphorus, which are vital for bone and muscle growth. Babies are born with a reserve of iron that will last for about six months; then they have to be given iron in solids or as supplements.

Trace elements: Minerals such as zinc, copper, and fluoride are essential to your baby's health. The first two are present in breast and formula milk, but fluoride, which protects against dental decay, is not. Never give fluoride supplements without checking with your midwife or doctor, as excessive amounts can cause fluorosis (discoloration of the tooth enamel).

Your milk supply

Look after yourself properly by staying relaxed, eating well, and drinking enough fluids, and you'll have more than enough milk for your baby.

✳ Rest as much as you can, particularly in the first weeks, and try to get plenty of sleep.

✳ Let the housework go; do only what is absolutely essential.

✳ Eat a well-balanced diet that is fairly rich in protein. Avoid highly refined carbohydrates such as cakes, biscuits, and sweets.

✳ Consult your doctor about taking iron and possibly some vitamin supplements.

✳ Drink fluids according to your thirst. Keep a drink by you while feeding if necessary.

✳ Expressing milk in between breastfeeds will encourage your breasts to produce more milk.

✳ The combined contraceptive pill can decrease milk supply, so avoid it while breastfeeding. The progesterone-only pill may be prescribed instead, but discuss methods of contraception with your doctor.

About breastfeeding

Breastfeeding has to be learned, so seek support and advice not just from your midwife or health visitor but also from family and friends with babies. Above all, you will learn from your baby by understanding and learning how to respond to her signals. Your breasts need no special preparation for feeding, but if you have an inverted nipple use a breast shell to make it protrude so that your baby can latch on to it. If you are having your baby in hospital, make sure the nursing staff know that you intend to breastfeed, and don't be reticent in asking for help. Suckle your baby from birth (in the delivery room, if you are in hospital) to bond with her as early as possible and to let her get used to suckling.

Colostrum and breast milk

Water, protein, and minerals make up the thin, yellow fluid called colostrum that the breasts produce during the 72 hours after delivery. Colostrum contains antibodies to protect the baby against intestinal and respiratory infections. In the first few days, encourage your baby to breastfeed frequently to increase her intake of colostrum and to stimulate the production of breastmilk. Frequent feeding also allows your baby to learn how to latch onto the breast effectively (see p. 40).

As your baby progresses through a feed, the milk changes from being thirst quenching to being more calorie-rich. So it is important to let your baby feed for as long as she wants from one breast before offering her the second if she is still hungry.

How the let-down reflex works
When your baby sucks at the breast, the sucking action sends messages to the hypothalamus, which in turn stimulates the pituitary gland in your brain to release two hormones: prolactin, which stimulates the milk glands to produce milk; and oxytocin, which causes milk to be expressed. This transfer happens within seconds and is commonly known as the let-down reflex – it is often associated with a tingling or warm sensation.

Relaxed positions for breastfeeding

It is important that you are comfortable while feeding. If you are sitting, keep your feet firmly on the ground and use pillows to support your arms and back. Lying down is ideal for night feeds when your baby is still very small. You may find a lying position best if you've had a Caesarean section or after an episiotomy, if sitting is uncomfortable.

Lying positions Breastfeeding positions in which you can lie down are a restful alternative to sitting ones and will keep a wriggling baby off a tender Caesarean incision.

Sitting position Make sure you feel comfortable. Support your back and arms with cushions if you get tired.

Supply and demand

Milk is produced in glands that are buried deep in the breast, not in its fatty tissue, so breast size is no indication of how much milk you can produce; even small breasts give a perfectly good supply.

Milk is produced according to demand: don't worry that you'll run out of milk if your baby feeds very often. Her sucking stimulates your breasts to produce milk. The more she feeds, the more milk they will produce – and vice versa. I'm against babies being fed by the clock so I don't want to show any kind of chart, but the table below may be helpful.

Nursing bras Always wear a supportive nursing bra that has front fastenings and wide straps; try it on before you buy it. Drop-front or zip-fastening bras are easy to undo with one hand while you hold your baby. A good bra will minimize discomfort if your breasts become sore.

How often will she feed? This is what may happen. At first your baby will feed little and often. By two months she will feed less frequently and take more at each feed than before.

TIME	2-WEEK OLD BABY	2-MONTH OLD BABY
12 midnight	√	
2 am	√	√
4 am		
6 am	√	
8 am		√
10 am	√	√
12 noon	√	
2 pm	√	√
4 pm	√	
6 pm	√	√
8 pm	√	√
10 pm	√	
12 midnight	√	

How long on each breast?

You should keep your baby on the breast for as long as she shows interest in sucking.

✳ If your baby continues to suck for a prolonged period of time, she is probably enjoying suckling and is still getting small amounts of milk. This is fine if it is not making your nipples sore, and will give your breasts the signals they need to produce more milk for this feed and the following ones.

✳ If your baby seems to want to suck more, gently take her off your nipple (see below right) when she has finished feeding from one breast and put her on the other. She may not suck for so long on the second breast.

Breastfeeding your baby

If feeding time is relaxed and pleasurable, breastfeeding creates a strong bond between mother and baby. Make sure your baby can see you. Smile and talk to her while she is suckling. She'll soon associate the pleasure of feeding with the sight of your face, the sound of your voice, and the smell of your skin. Make sure you are both comfortable before you start (see p. 39). If your baby still seems hungry after feeding from one breast, offer the other breast, winding her before changing over (see p. 51). Alternate the first breast you offer at each feed. You can put a safety pin on your bra to remind you which breast was last suckled.

Recognizing common problems

It is perfectly normal for breastfeeding not to go smoothly at first, so be patient and don't get anxious about minor setbacks. Remember that your baby is learning too and that it may take time for both of you to get used to each other. Consult your midwife or health visitor for advice. Don't forget there are many sources of support for breastfeeding mothers, such as the National Childbirth Trust (NCT), the Breastfeeding Network, the Association of Breastfeeding Mothers, and La Leche League. There is also an NHS National Breastfeeding Helpline (see p. 93).

Breastfeeding

1 Getting her attention Your baby should open her mouth as soon as she smells your milk. You can stroke the side of her cheek to stimulate the rooting reflex, which causes her to turn towards your breast, open-mouthed.

2 Latching on Your baby should take the nipple and much of the areola into her mouth. It should feel comfortable once she has settled into her feed, as the nipple should be resting against the soft palate at the back of her mouth. If it is painful, try again.

3 Releasing the nipple To break the suction, slip your little finger into the corner of the baby's mouth. Your breast will slip out easily instead of being dragged out.

Refusing the breast It is usual for a newborn not to suck very vigorously or for very long during her first 24 to 36 hours. If this happens later, however, there may be a problem. Breathing difficulties are the most likely reason for a baby to be having problems. It may be that your breast is covering her nostrils; if so, gently pull the breast away from the baby's face, just above the areola. If her nose seems to be snuffly or blocked, consult your doctor, who may prescribe nose drops to clear the nostrils.

If there's no obvious cause for your baby's refusal to feed, she may just be fretful. A baby who's been crying with hunger or been changed, fussed over, or played with when hungry, can become too distressed to take the breast. You'll need to soothe her by holding her firmly and talking or singing to her.

If there has been delay in starting to breastfeed (as with a premature baby who has had to be bottlefed), your baby may find it more difficult to take the breast, and you will have to be patient. Your midwife or health visitor will advise you whether to give expressed milk from a special cup until the baby can take all she needs from the breast. Supplementary bottles (see p. 43) are rarely necessary, and may cause mothers to give up breastfeeding. Your own expressed milk is a better alternative.

Comfort sucking You'll learn to tell the difference between actual feeding and comfort sucking. During a feed, you may notice that your baby is sucking strongly but not swallowing. If your nipples are not sore, your baby can suck for as long as she wants, although she takes most of her feed in the first few minutes. Frequent suckling is a good way of stimulating your milk supply and a great way to meet your baby's needs.

Sleeping through feeds If your baby seems to have little interest in food during the first few days, make sure that she takes as much as she wants from one breast. If she sleeps at the breast, it means that she is contented, although premature babies, who sleep a lot, need to be woken and fed regularly. If your baby does fall asleep at the breast, wake her gently half an hour later and offer a feed; if she is hungry, she will perk up.

Fretful feeding If your baby doesn't settle down to feed, or appears not to be satisfied, she is probably just sucking and not getting enough milk. This may lead to sore nipples. Check that your baby is properly latched on and has a good proportion of the areola in her mouth.

Is my baby underfeeding?

You may feel anxious that you can't see how much your baby has taken, but it is rare for a breastfed baby not to get enough milk. Remember, though, that it does take time for both mothers and babies to get the hang of breastfeeding.

* If your baby wants to continue sucking even though she's finished feeding from both breasts, this doesn't always signify hunger; she may just enjoy sucking.

* If she seems fretful and hungry, have her weighed at your baby clinic to check if she is gaining weight as quickly as expected. If you are at all worried about your baby's feeding, contact your health visitor or doctor.

Tips for expressing milk

Make expressing milk as easy on yourself as possible, and take care to store the milk correctly.

✳ Leaning over a low surface while expressing may give you backache. Have the container at a convenient height.

✳ Expressing milk should be painless. If it hurts, stop at once. Ask your health visitor to check you are doing it correctly.

✳ The more relaxed you are, the easier it will be to express. If the milk doesn't flow, place a warm flannel over your breasts to open the ducts, or try expressing while in the bath. Alternatively, express from one breast at the same time as you breastfeed your baby from the other.

✳ If you're concerned that your baby might not go back to breastfeeding after getting used to the bottle's teat, try feeding her from a specially designed cup, or spooning her the expressed milk from a cup with a spoon. Your hands must be clean and all equipment and containers should be sterile.

✳ Refrigerate then freeze your breast milk as soon as you've collected it. Breast milk keeps for three days in the fridge if it is between 5–10°C and for six months in a freezer at −18°C or below.

✳ Store expressed milk in sterile, sealable containers. Sterile plastic bottle liners are ideal.

Expressing milk

You can store expressed milk in the refrigerator or freezer. This helps you feel less tied down by breastfeeding, allows your baby to be fed with your milk if you need to go out, and gives your partner the chance to share in the feeding.

Express milk by hand or with a manual or electric breast pump; hand expressing may be the easiest and most convenient method. Before starting, you will need a bowl, a funnel, and a container that can be sealed. Sterilize all the equipment in a sterilizing solution or with boiling water or in a special steam unit, and wash your hands before you begin.

In the first six weeks, hand expressing is nearly always a bit difficult as the breasts might not have reached full production, but don't give up. Because breasts produce milk in response to demand, you may need to express milk in order to keep your supply going – if your baby is premature and can't breastfeed yet, for instance. Even if you use a pump, it is worth learning the technique of hand expressing in case you need it. You can express at any time of the day or night, so discover for yourself what time suits you best.

Expressing by pump

All pumps work on suction and comprise a funnel or shield, a pump mechanism, and a container. The assembly and operation of the different brands of pump will vary a little, so follow the manufacturer's instructions.

Using pumps Fit the funnel over your areola to form an airtight seal, then operate the pump to express milk. Electric pumps (below) imitate a baby's sucking cycle more closely than manual pumps (right) and are best if you need to express often.

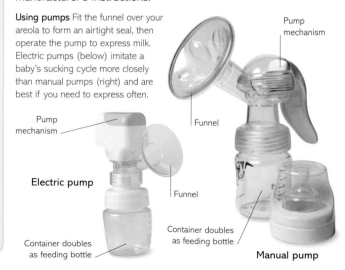

Pump mechanism

Pump mechanism

Funnel

Funnel

Electric pump

Container doubles as feeding bottle

Container doubles as feeding bottle

Manual pump

Expressing by hand

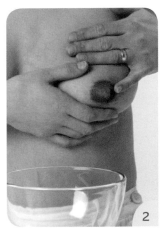

1 Feel around your breasts, working back from the nipple until you find an area that feels different.

2 Gently squeeze this area with your thumb and finger, then release. If it hurts, you are being too rough.

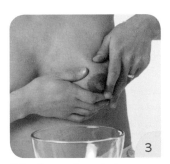

3 Keeping your fingers in the same place on the breast, continue to squeeze and release the breast in rhythm until milk begins to flow. Be patient, as this may take time at first.

4 If you are unable to produce a flow of milk, try altering the position of your fingers slightly, or try a gentle all-over breast massage before returning to rhythmic squeezing.

5 Switch to the other breast when the flow slows down, and keep switching back and forth between the two breasts until both are empty.

Supplementary feeds

There may be times, such as when you have a blocked duct or a very sore nipple, when it is painful to breastfeed.

Hard as it is, it's best to avoid offering formula if you possibly can. There are many benefits to your baby being exclusively breastfed for the first six months if possible. When feeding is painful, express milk from the affected breast and offer this from a small cup or beaker. Giving supplementary formula feeds can undermine the production of breast milk.

A baby who has become used to the nipple may dislike plastic teats. Unfortunately, it can be difficult to tell whether your baby just dislikes the teat or is not hungry. She'll get used to the bottle if you persist, but you may then find that she doesn't want to go back to the breast. If this happens, try giving milk from a sterilized spoon or cup.

Help for sore nipples

Suckling your baby can cause soreness around the nipples. The following tips may help to minimize any problems.

✱ Always make sure that your baby has the nipple and areola well into her mouth.

✱ Always take your baby off the breast gently (see p. 40).

✱ Treat your breasts completely normally during breastfeeding and in between sessions of breastfeeding, unless you have a cracked nipple, in which case you can apply white soft paraffin or Lansinoh to the nipple between feeds.

✱ Make sure your nipples are dry before putting your bra back on after a feed.

✱ If one of your nipples does become sore, it may be due to poor positioning or your baby not latching on properly. Ask your health visitor's advice on correct positioning (also see pp. 40–41).

✱ You may want to try a soft silicone nipple shield, which should be sterilized before each use, but seek advice from a midwife or health visitor before using one as they can mask a deeper problem, and they can interfere with effective feeding.

Managing breastfeeding

Breastfeeding may go smoothly right from the start, but it is also normal at first for you to be a bit clumsy, for the baby not to suck for very long, or for your breasts to be a bit sore. Learning takes time, so be patient until things get easier.

Care of the breasts

Treat your breasts during breastfeeding as you would normally. You may find a bra provides useful support, but don't wear one if it is uncomfortable. A proper nursing bra can be very useful as it allows access for feeding, but your own comfort should decide what you wear.

Once your milk flow is established the milk may leak out quite a lot. Use breast pads or clean handkerchiefs inside your bra to soak it up, and change these frequently for cleanliness. A plastic breast shell with a reservoir will help to keep your nipples dry and catch the leaks of milk. Wash and sterilize the shell before reusing.

What happens if you are ill

It is important to try to continue feeding even while you are ill. This will ensure you keep up an adequate milk supply and can pass antibodies to your child that will protect her from any infection you may have. If you are confined to bed you can express milk so that your partner can feed the baby when you are not feeling up to it. If you are too ill even to express your milk, then your baby can be given formula milk by bottle or by spoon and, although she may not like this at first, she will take the milk as she becomes more and more hungry.

You can still breastfeed if you have to go into hospital. Inform the nursing staff as soon as possible that this is what you intend to do, so they have time to make the necessary arrangements: for instance, someone will have to be on hand to lift and change your baby if you are too tired or ill to do so. If you have an operation, however, you will not be able to breastfeed afterwards because of the anaesthetic – you'll be too groggy and, more importantly, the drugs you have been given will have passed into your milk. If you know you'll be having an operation, try to express and freeze milk so that your baby can be bottlefed until you have recovered. It will take several days for your usual milk supply to return, but by letting your baby suckle as frequently as possible, this will happen sooner rather than later.

What to do if problems arise

Over the months of breastfeeding, problems may arise if, for instance, your baby is not latching on properly or drags on the nipple as she comes off (see p. 40). Keep your breasts clean and dry, wear a proper nursing bra, and act at once if your nipple starts feeling sore or becomes cracked.

Cracked nipple If not dealt with properly, sore nipples may become cracked and you'll feel a shooting pain as your baby suckles. Keep feeding if at all possible. Follow the advice on p. 44, and if necessary, express milk by hand; it can be fed to your baby by bottle or from a special cup. Your midwife or health visitor should be able to give you advice.

Engorgement Towards the end of the first week of breastfeeding (before it is properly established), your breasts may become over full, and painful and quite hard to the touch, and your baby won't be able to latch on successfully. Make sure you wear a good nursing bra to minimize discomfort and gently express some milk (see pp. 42–43) before feeding to relieve the fullness. This will also help your baby latch on more easily. Having warm baths will also help to relieve the discomfort by encouraging your milk to flow.

Blocked duct Tight clothing or engorgement can cause a milk duct to become blocked, resulting in a hard red patch on the outside of the breast where the duct lies. Prevent this by feeding often and encouraging your baby to empty your breasts; check that your bra fits properly, too. If you do get a blocked duct, feed often, and offer the affected breast first.

Mastitis A blocked duct that is not treated can lead to an acute infection: mastitis. The breast will be inflamed and a red patch will appear on the outside, and you may experience flu-like symptoms. You need to empty the breast, so go on breastfeeding. Your doctor may prescribe antibiotics to clear up the infection.

Breast abscess An untreated blocked duct or mastitis can result in a breast abscess. You may feel feverish and have a tender, shiny red patch on your breast. If treatment with antibiotics fails, the abscess needs to be drained surgically. You may be able to continue breastfeeding even if you need this minor operation – ask your doctor's advice.

Medicines and breastfeeding

If you can, avoid all drugs when you are breastfeeding. Many medications pass from your body into the breast milk and can affect your baby.

* If you are already taking medication or you need to consult your doctor about new problems, always tell her that you are breastfeeding.

* Ask your doctor or family planning clinic for advice in helping you choose the method of contraception that is best and most suitable for you.

* If you want to breastfeed and use oral contraceptives, it's probably best to take the progestogen-only "mini-pill", as the oestrogen in the combined pill is thought to reduce your supply of milk.

Bottles and milk

Milk formulas

A variety of milk formulas is available, all with carefully balanced ingredients to make them as close as possible to breast milk; in fact, formula milk has added vitamin D and iron, levels of which are quite low in breast milk.

Most formulas are based on cows' milk. Some are available both in powder and ready-mixed forms. There are soya-based formulas available, but never give these to your baby without the advice of your doctor or midwife.

Ready-mixed milk in cartons or ready-to-feed bottles is ultra-heat treated (UHT), which means the milk is sterile and will keep in a cool place until the "best before" or "sell by" date. Once a carton has been opened, the milk will keep for 24 hours in the refrigerator. Ready-mixed milk is more expensive than powdered formula, but it is convenient – you may like to use it when travelling.

If you use powdered formula, it's essential that you make it up precisely according to the manufacturer's instructions. Some parents are tempted to add extra powder to make the milk "more nourishing". If you do this, your baby will get too much protein and fat, and not enough water. If you add too little powder, your baby will not be getting the nutrients she needs for healthy growth.

Many babies will be bottlefed at some stage – if not continuously right from the start, then often after weaning or with supplementary bottles. New infant formulas, bottles, and teats come into the market regularly, all with the aim of making bottlefeeding as convenient and as similar to breastfeeding as possible.

If you bottlefeed from birth, the one important thing you cannot give your baby is colostrum (see p. 38), so even if you're not intending to continue breastfeeding your baby, you'll be giving her the best possible start if you put her to the breast for the first few days. If you decide not to do this (or for some reason you cannot), the hospital staff will take care of your baby's first feeds.

One feature of bottlefeeding is that the new father can be just as involved as the new mother at feeding times. Make sure that your partner feeds your baby as soon as possible after the birth. This way he can get used to the technique and won't be worried about handling her. He should let the baby nestle up to his bare skin when she feeds, to help her bond with him.

Bottles and teats

There is a range of different feeding bottles and teats now available. You may need to try a few to find out what suits your baby best (below are some examples).

Tapered bottle

Waisted bottle

Easy-grip bottle

Disposable bottle

Cleaning bottles and teats

Cleaning the bottles Scrub the insides of bottles with a bottle brush and rub teats well to remove any traces of milk. Rinse thoroughly.

Sterilizing You should follow the manufacturer's instructions for your model of sterilizer, and cool the equipment before using.

Sterilizing the bottles

It is a good idea to practise with your feeding equipment before you go into hospital, so buy it well in advance of your delivery date. Large department stores and pharmacies sell bottlefeeding packs that have all the essential equipment. Keep your sterilizing equipment in the kitchen, preferably near the sink.

To use the cold-water sterilizing method with sterilizing tablets, fill the unit with cold water up to the guide mark, then dissolve one or two tablets in the water, according to the manufacturer's instructions. Clean the bottles and teats as described above, then put them with the measuring scoop and knife into the unit, making sure that all the equipment is submerged (fill the bottles with water so that they stay under the sterilizing solution and don't bob about). Leave the equipment for the required time and rinse in recently boiled water that has cooled down; drain when you are ready to use it.

The majority of sterilizing units usually hold only four to six bottles. Your newborn baby, however, will be taking something like seven feeds over 24 hours, so you may have to sterilize the bottles twice a day – morning and evening – to make sure that you have enough to make up a feed whenever she is hungry. After the feed, rinse the bottle in warm water and put it aside. It is wise to continue sterilizing all milk-feeding equipment until your baby is a year old.

Sterilizing methods

Cold-water sterilization and boiling are both effective methods. It is as well to be aware of other methods in case you're away from home, or run out of tablets to use in a sterilizing unit.

✳ A simple sterilizing method is to wash the equipment and boil it for at least 10 minutes in a large, covered pan.

✳ Alternatively, put all the equipment into a large, covered plastic container and use sterilizing tablets (or fluid) and cold water.

✳ Steam sterilizing units quickly and effectively destroy bacteria on your equipment.

✳ You can sterilize the feeding equipment in a microwave, using a specially designed steam unit, as long as the equipment is suitable for microwave use.

✳ Once your baby is more than 12 months old, you can wash feeding equipment in a dishwasher. Clean teats before they go in. Run the dishwasher on the normal cycle.

Milk flow from the teat

The hole in the teat should be large enough to let the milk flow in a stream of several drops per second when the bottle is inverted.

Too large a hole means your baby will get too much too fast and splutter; too small, and she will get tired before she is satisfied. You can buy teats with holes of different sizes that allow the milk to flow faster or slower. Make sure you buy the correct size for your baby's needs.

Choose sculpted teats – these are best because they are shaped to fit the baby's palate, allowing her control over the flow.

Measuring out Using the scoop provided, measure out the quantities accurately. Use the back of a sterilized knife blade to level off the powder in the scoop exactly.

Bottlefeeding your baby

Before you start giving your baby a bottle feed, it is essential to bear in mind a few essential points: the formula must be properly made up, using the specified quantities, so that your baby gets the correct balance of both nutrients and water; the formula must be prepared in such a way that it remains hygienic and safe for your baby; and your baby should be able to draw milk at a comfortable rate from the bottle. You should not store made-up formula milk, as this increases the chances that bacteria will multiply and make your baby ill. Throw away milk that has been left standing for more than two hours.

Making up formula
Equipment
✳ Bottle
✳ Knife
✳ Measuring scoop from formula pack
✳ Teat and cap

Sterilizing It is important to sterilize all your equipment between feeds. There are several types of sterilizer in the market (see p. 47), so choose the one that works best for you and follow the manufacturer's instructions.

Clean and disinfect the surface you are going to use and wash your hands. Fill the kettle with clean, fresh tap water, boil it, and allow it to cool to 70°C (158°F) by leaving it in the kettle for no more than 30 minutes.

Measuring Pour the correct amount of hot water into the bottle first. Using the scoop provided with your pack, measure out the required amount of formula and add it to the water in the bottle. Use a plastic knife to level off each scoop and don't pack the formula down in the scoop. Never add extra formula when making up bottles or the milk will be too concentrated and could be dangerous for your baby.

Mixing Put the cap and teat on the bottle and shake the bottle well until you're sure there are no lumps or residue and the formula mixture is smooth. Cool the bottle to a safe temperature by holding it – with a cap covering the teat – under cold running water.

Giving a bottle feed

Make yourself comfortable, with your arms well supported. Hold your baby half-sitting with her head in the crook of your elbow and her back along your forearm – this will allow her to swallow safely and easily. Keep your face close to hers and chat to her all the time. Or you may like to try other positions (see p. 39) until you discover which one suits you both best.

You should have already tested the flow of the milk (see p. 48). If it is difficult for your baby to draw the milk, gently remove the bottle from her mouth so that air can enter the bottle, then continue as before. Hold the bottle at a slight angle so that the milk covers the teat completely and your baby does not swallow air with the milk as she sucks.

Bottlefeeding

1 **Testing milk temperature** Before you begin feeding, cool the bottle and test the heat of the milk. Try a few drops on your wrist; it should feel neither hot nor cold to the touch.

2 **Giving the bottle** Gently stroke your baby's nearest cheek to elicit her sucking reflex. Insert the teat carefully into her mouth. If you push the teat too far in, she may gag on it.

3 **Make feeding times pleasant** Chat to your baby and smile at her while feeding. Let her pause mid-feed; change her onto the other arm to give her a new view and your arm a rest.

4 **Removing the bottle** If you want your baby to release the bottle, gently slide your little finger into the corner of her mouth. This will break the suction on the teat.

Bottlefeeding routines

As formula milk differs from breast milk in its balance of proteins, it takes longer to digest compared to breast milk. In the early days, this means that bottlefed babies tend to go for longer between feeds. However, the principles of feeding are exactly the same: feed your baby on demand. When your baby is born, she is unlikely to take much over 60 millilitres (2 fluid ounces) at each feed, but as she grows she will take fewer and larger feeds.

Never feed your baby according to the clock: allow her to determine when she is to be fed. She will let you know quite clearly with her cries when she is hungry. Your baby's appetite will vary, so if she seems satisfied, let her leave what she does not want. Don't feel that your baby has to finish the bottle at each feed. She will only get too full and posset it back (see p. 52) or – worse – become overfed and fat. On the other hand, if your baby is still hungry, give her some extra milk from another bottle. If this happens regularly, start to make more milk for every feed.

Night feeds

Your baby will need feeding at least once during the night. This break in your sleep, on top of all the other things that you have to do to take care of her, may make you extremely tired and tense. The problem is not so much the number of hours' sleep that you lose, but more the way in which your sleep patterns are broken over long periods. For this reason, it is very important that you get adequate rest, day and night. If you are doing most of the feeding, try to get your partner to take on some of the other jobs.

Reducing night feeds

At first, five hours is the longest time your baby will be able to sleep without being woken by hunger. Once she reaches a weight of around 5 kilograms (11 pounds), try to stretch the time between feeds with the aim of making sure that you are getting about six hours of undisturbed sleep at night. Although your baby will have her own routine, it's sensible to try to time her last feed to coincide with your own bedtime, which should be as late as possible. You may find that your baby will still wake up and demand the early morning feed, no matter how much you try to change her routine. If this happens, you'll just have to be patient, make the night feeds as comfortable as possible, and look forward to when she drops the early morning feed.

Overfeeding

Chubby babies can look cuddly and attractive, but fat cells, once produced, can't be removed, and a fat baby may grow into a fat adult, with all the attendant risks to health. Sadly, it is easy to overfeed a bottlefed baby. The reasons for this are twofold: first, it is tempting to put extra formula into the bottle, but you should always follow the instructions precisely (see p. 48), otherwise you'll be giving the baby calories that are not needed. Second, in your anxiety to feed your baby "properly", you'll want to see her finish the last drop of the feed, but you should always let her decide when she has finished. Giving sweet, syrupy drinks and introducing solids too early can also cause overfeeding. Research clearly suggests that breastfed babies are much less likely to become obese. It is thought that this is because they are able to moderate their energy requirements day to day and develop an innate sense of when they are full.

Underfeeding

It is rare for bottlefed babies to be underfed. You should feed your baby on demand and not at set times, and you will find that demands vary from day to day. If you insist on feeding according to a schedule, never giving extra milk, and refusing interim feeds even when your baby is crying for them, then she won't get all the milk that she needs.

If your baby seems fretful time and again after she drains each bottle, she may well be hungry. In this case, offer her an extra 60 millilitres (2 fluid ounces) of formula. If she takes it, then she needs it.

You may find that your baby demands frequent feeds but doesn't take much: this could be because the teat hole is too small (see p. 48), so that she is having difficulty sucking the milk and becomes tired with sucking before she gets enough.

Winding

Winding releases any air that your baby may have swallowed during feeding or in crying prior to feeding. Babies vary greatly in their reaction to wind and it's unlikely to cause discomfort; many babies are not noticeably happier or more contented

Hygiene and preparation

Your baby needs protection from bacteria, so make sure that all feeding equipment is scrupulously clean, and take care with the preparation of formula.

* Read and follow sterilizing instructions carefully.

* Wash your hands before you sterilize the equipment, prepare bottles, or give feeds.

* Never add extra formula: follow the instructions closely.

* Give the milk to your baby as soon as it has been prepared.

* Throw away milk left over after a feed.

How to wind Hold your baby close to you. Gently but firmly stroke or pat her back to help her bring up any bubbles of air.

after being winded. Swallowing air is more common in bottlefed babies, but you can prevent it to some extent by tilting the bottle more as your baby empties it, so that the teat is full of milk and not air, or by using disposable bottles. The one real point in favour of winding your baby, whether you are breastfeeding or bottlefeeding, is that it makes you pause, relax, slow down, hold your baby gently, and stroke or pat her reassuringly, and this is good for both of you. Therefore, the way I look at winding is this: by all means do it, if only for your own peace of mind, but don't become fanatical about it.

Possetting

If your baby tends to posset, that is, regurgitate milk (some babies never do), you may wonder if she's keeping enough down. My youngest son was a child who tended to posset, and I worried in case he wasn't getting enough to eat. I simply followed my own instinct, which was to offer him more food. When he didn't take it, I assumed that he had possetted an excess that he didn't need. The commonest cause of possetting in very young babies is overfeeding, and this is another reason why you should never insist that your bottlefed baby finishes her feed.

Forcible vomiting – where the milk is projected out of the baby's mouth with force – should be reported right away to your doctor, especially if it occurs consistently after several feeds. Vomiting in a small baby is always very serious because it can quickly lead to dehydration, and you should seek medical advice as soon as possible.

Chapter 4

Bathing, changing, and dressing

Caring for your baby means looking after her hygiene and physical comfort as well as her dietary needs. Keeping your baby clean at first involves a seemingly endless round of nappies, but this stage will pass.

Washing a girl

There is no need to open the lips of your baby girl's vulva to clean inside; indeed, you should never try to do so. Just wash the skin of the nappy area and dry it carefully.

When washing your baby girl, take care to wipe from front to back (in other words, towards the anus) when you clean the nappy area. This will avoid soiling the vulva and minimize the risk of spreading bacteria from the bowels to the bladder, which could cause infection.

Bathing and hygiene

Part of your daily routine will be to keep your baby clean. Many new parents worry about handling a very small baby in the baby bath, but you will soon get used to bathtime and look forward to it as an opportunity to have fun and play with your baby. Instead of feeling apprehensive, set aside half an hour, have everything you need around you, try to relax, and you will enjoy it.

A young baby doesn't need bathing very often because only his bottom, face, neck, and skin creases get dirty, so you need to bathe him only every two or three days; in between times, you can just top and tail him (see below). This allows you to attend to the parts of your baby that really need washing with as little disturbance and distress to him as possible. You should use cooled, boiled water for a newborn, but when your baby is a little older (at about one month), you can use warm water straight from the tap. Do wash your baby's hair often to prevent cradle cap from forming (see p. 57); the act of washing removes any scales. You needn't use soap for a newborn; after about six weeks, bath lotion, soap, or other baby toiletries are fine.

Babies don't like having their skin exposed to the air, so while you are washing your baby, keep him undressed for as short a time as possible. Warm a big, fluffy towel on a not-too-hot radiator and have it ready to wrap your baby in as soon as you are finished.

Topping and tailing your baby

1 Face and ears Using cooled, boiled water, moisten a piece of cotton wool and gently wipe your baby's face. Wipe the eyes from the bridge of the nose outwards. Clean outside and behind the ears.

2 Hands and feet Clean your baby's hands and feet with fresh pieces of cotton wool and then dry them thoroughly with a soft towel. (A facecloth is fine when your baby is older.)

Body care Once you have taken care of your baby's nappy area and made sure that his skin is kept free from any traces of food or dirt that might cause irritation, the rest will take care of itself.

Eyes, nose, and ears Wipe your baby's eyes with balls of cotton wool and cooled, boiled water. Work from the inner part of the eye to the outer, using a fresh piece of cotton wool for each eye to avoid spreading any infection.

Don't poke around inside your baby's nose and ears; they are self-cleaning, so don't use ear or nose drops except on your doctor's advice. Just clean his ears with moist cotton wool. If you see wax in your baby's ears, don't try to scrape it out. It is a natural secretion of the canal of the outer ear, is antiseptic, and protects the eardrum from dust and grit. Removing it will simply cause the ear to produce more wax. If you are really concerned, consult your doctor.

Nails Keep your newborn baby's nails short so he does not scratch his skin. The best time to cut them is after a bath, when they are soft; use a pair of small, blunt-ended scissors.

Navel During the few days after birth, the umbilical stump dries, shrivels, and drops off (see p. 13). You can bathe your baby before the stump has healed, but do dry it thoroughly afterwards. Allow the area to stay open to the air as much as possible to help speed up the shrinking and healing process.

Washing a boy

Never pull back your baby boy's foreskin for cleaning; it's quite tight at this stage and could get stuck (by the time he is three or four, the foreskin will be loose and can be retracted without force). Wash the whole of the nappy area and dry carefully, particularly the skin creases.

If your baby has just been circumcised, watch carefully for any signs of bleeding. A few drops of blood are normal. Slight inflammation and swelling are also normal, and these will settle down in a short while.

If bleeding persists, however, or if there is any sign of infection, consult your doctor. Make sure to get advice about bathing, taking care of the penis, and what to do about the dressing if one has been applied.

3

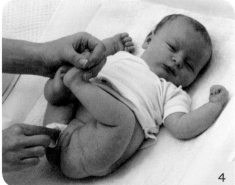

4

3 **Wet nappy** Gently remove your baby's nappy. If it's just wet rather than soiled, wipe the nappy area with cotton wool, dampened with warm water. Babies like to stay dry, so change nappies frequently.

4 **Soiled nappy** Remove as much of the faeces as you can when you take off the nappy, and clean the area gently and thoroughly with water and cotton wool (see p. 64). Keep a finger between the ankles to stop them rubbing together.

Use of toiletries

A newborn's skin is delicate. You should not use soap or wipes until your baby is at least six weeks old – these remove the natural oils from his skin and leave it dry and uncomfortable. Special baby toiletries are mild and will not irritate your baby's skin; many of them are hypoallergenic, too.

✳ A little baby oil in your baby's bath water is a good moisturizer for very dry skin.

✳ For cleaning delicate skin, such as the nappy area, it's best to use only water.

✳ Never use talcum powder on the skin creases because it can cake in the creases and cause irritation.

✳ Zinc and castor oil cream or petroleum jelly are waterproof and will protect your baby's skin from urine. Medicated nappy creams containing titanium salts are good if your baby has nappy rash (see p. 67).

Giving a sponge bath

If your baby really hates being undressed, or if you are a bit daunted by giving him a bath, a sponge bath is the answer. Hold your baby securely on your lap while removing the least amount of clothing at any time. If you find it hard to manoeuvre your baby while he is on your lap, put him on a changing mat and follow the same sponge bath method, taking care to keep one half covered while washing the other. Put a bowl of warm water near you before you begin.

Sponge bath

1 Upper body Sit your baby on a towel on your lap. Holding him firmly, undress the top half of his body and wash his front with a sponge or soft cloth. Pat him dry.

2 Washing the back After washing the front of your baby, lean him gently forward over your arm and wash his back. Use a soft towel to dry him thoroughly.

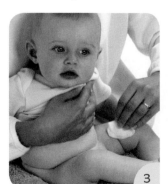

3 Nappy area or hair wash Either wash your baby's hair at this stage, or dress his top half in clean clothes and remove his lower clothing and nappy. Clean the nappy area (see p. 64).

4 Lower body Use the sponge or cloth to wash his legs and feet. Pat dry, put on barrier cream (if you use it) and a clean nappy, and dress him.

Hair care and washing

From birth, you can wash your baby's hair daily, but don't feel you have to use shampoo: bath lotion dissolved in water will do. After about 12–16 weeks, wash his hair with water daily and once or twice a week with baby shampoo. Choose a non-sting variety, but do still take care to avoid getting it near his eyes. For a small baby, you can tuck his legs under your arm while supporting his back and cradling his head (see p. 58); or sit on the edge of the bath with your baby across your legs, facing you, to make him feel secure if he's scared of water. Don't be nervous about the fontanelles (see p. 12) – the membrane covering them is very tough, and there is no need to scrub his hair, so you can do no harm if you are gentle.

Apply the shampoo or bath lotion to your baby's hair and gradually work it in until a lather forms. Wait for about 15 seconds before rinsing it off; there is no need to apply it a second time. To rinse the hair, just use a flannel dipped in warm water to wipe away the suds; do your best to remove every trace of soap. When drying your baby's hair, try not to cover his face or he may panic and start to cry. It is best just to use the end of the towel to avoid this.

If your baby dislikes hair washing

Many babies hate having their hair washed, even if they enjoy having a bath. In this case, it may be best to keep hair washing separate from bathtime. If your child associates the two, he may start to fuss about taking baths as well.

The main reason for dislike of hair washing is that babies hate getting water and soap in their eyes, so try to avoid this as far as you can. Specially designed shields are available that fit around the hairline and prevent water and suds from running down your baby's face while you rinse his hair. You may also find that your baby will become less distressed if you hold him in your lap while washing his hair (facing you so that he feels more secure), and use a flannel to wet and rinse his hair rather than pouring water over his head.

Never try to force the issue, and never forcibly hold your baby still while you wash his hair. If hair washing is clearly causing him great distress, give up for two or three weeks before trying again. You can still keep his hair reasonably clean by sponging it with warm water to remove any food or dirt, or brushing it out with a soft, damp brush. The hair will probably become greasy, but this will not do any harm.

What is cradle cap?

Occasionally, you may see yellowy, scaly patches on your baby's scalp. Cradle cap is extremely common and is not caused by poor hygiene or any shampoo you are using. It generally disappears after a few weeks.

Gently washing your newborn baby's scalp every day with a very soft bristle brush and a little baby shampoo in warm water will prevent cradle cap from forming. Even if he has very little hair, brush through it so that scales cannot form.

If cradle cap does appear, smear a little olive oil on his scalp at night to soften and loosen the scales, making them easy to wash away the next morning. Don't be tempted to pick them off with your finger nail: doing so will just irritate the scalp.

Cradle cap Scaly patches of cradle cap on a baby's scalp are not harmful and usually clear up on their own accord after a few weeks. If cradle cap does persist, check with your health visitor, who may recommend a special shampoo.

Bathing tips for your baby

Make bathtimes as pleasant and enjoyable as possible so that you and your baby will look forward to them.

✽ Before you start, make sure that you have everything that you need close at hand.

✽ Always put cold water into the bath first. Test the final temperature with your elbow or the inner side of your wrist.

✽ Keep the water in the bath shallow: about 5–8 centimetres (2–3 inches) is deep enough.

✽ Have your baby undressed for the minimum time: small babies quickly become cold.

✽ Wear a waterproof apron to protect your clothing; a plastic-backed towelling one will feel nicer against your baby's skin.

✽ Put a towel on a radiator to warm, but don't let the towel get too hot.

✽ There is no need to add soap or lotion products to bath water for very young infants.

Giving a bath

You can bathe your baby in any room that is warm, has no draughts, and has enough space to lay out all the equipment you need. If the bathroom is too cold or draughty, you can fill the baby's bath there or in the kitchen and then carry it to the chosen room (this won't work if it's too heavy).

A small baby can be washed in a plastic baby bath with a non-slip surface, specially designed for the purpose. Place the bath on a large worktop or table of a convenient height (usually about hip height) so that you don't have to bend too much; this will protect your back from unnecessary strain. Some baby baths come with their stands or are designed to straddle a full-sized bath tub. Either of these will make bathing your baby a far more comfortable task.

Giving your baby a bath

1 Testing the water temperature Use your elbow or the inner side of your wrist to test the water; it should be neither very hot nor very cold. Using a bath thermometer may be a help at first. It should register a temperature of 29.4°C (85°F).

2 Before the bath Undress your baby, clean his nappy area (see pp. 64–65), then wrap him in a towel. Clean his face and ears (see p. 54).

3 Washing his head Holding your baby as shown above, lean over the bath and wash his head. Rinse well and gently pat dry.

4 Putting him in the bath Support your baby's shoulders with one hand, tucking your fingers under his armpit, and support his legs or bottom with the other. Keep smiling and talking to him as you place him in the bath.

5 Washing Keep one hand beneath your baby's shoulders when you are washing him so that his head and his shoulders are always out of the water; use your free hand to wash him.

6 Lifting him out When your baby is clean and well rinsed, lift him out gently, supporting his shoulders and legs or bottom in the same way you did when putting him into the bath.

Baby's fear of bathing

Some babies are terrified of having a bath. Don't force your baby to remain in the water if he's frightened. Try again after a couple of days, using only a little water in the bath. In the meantime, give sponge baths (see p. 56) or just top and tail your baby (see p. 54).

If your baby continues to be frightened of water, you can try introducing it in a play context. Fill a large bowl and place it in a warm room (not the bathroom). Place a towel near it, and put toys into the bowl. Undress your baby and encourage him to play with the toys. If he seems happy doing this, let him splash in the water while you keep a grip on him.

After you've done this a few times, put a baby bath in place of the bowl and go on letting your baby play. When he tries to get into the water with the toys, you'll know he's lost his fear of water. However, be patient, and let him do this once or twice before you wash him in the bath.

7 Drying Wrap your baby in a towel and dry him thoroughly. Don't use talcum powder at all as it could gather in the skin creases and cause irritation.

Kidney and bladder function

Once food has been absorbed into the bloodstream, waste is removed from blood by the kidneys and eliminated from the body as urine.

Urine production Waste chemicals in the blood are removed and dissolved in water by the kidneys. The urine then passes down the ureters and into the bladder.

Voiding Urine is temporarily stored in the bladder, which is emptied through the urethra from time to time. Your baby won't be aware of passing urine until he's about 15–18 months. The feeling of wanting to pass urine comes some months later, because the infant bladder is able to hold urine for only a few minutes.

Bladder and bowel

A newborn baby can need up to 10 nappy changes a day. The frequency of changes will decrease, but most babies do not achieve a degree of bladder and bowel control until the second year. Although you can't speed up this process, your help and support will be very important to your child.

Passing urine

A young baby's bladder will empty itself automatically and frequently, during both the day and the night. As soon as it contains a little urine, the bladder wall stretches and the emptying action is stimulated. This is entirely normal, and your baby cannot be expected to behave differently, at least until the bladder has developed sufficiently to hold urine for longer periods of time.

Bowel movements

Once your baby settles into a regular routine, his stools will become firmer and paler (in the 24 hours after delivery, he will have passed a sticky black substance called meconium). You don't need to pay much attention to his stools, and you certainly should never become obsessive or worried about them as long as your baby is content and thriving.

The number of stools a baby passes varies greatly, and initially most bottlefed babies pass a stool for every feed. On the other hand, a breastfed baby may pass only one stool or less a day because there is little waste. The frequency of his bowel motions gradually decreases as your baby gets older. In the beginning, your baby may pass a stool five or six times a day, but after three or four weeks he may be having only about two movements a day. This is quite normal and should cause you no worry. Similarly, the odd loose, unformed stool or totally green stool is very typical of a young baby's bowel movements, and should be no cause for concern unless looseness persists beyond 24 hours. In this case, you should seek your doctor's advice.

Changes in bowel movements

Don't worry if your baby's stools look different from one day to the next. It is quite normal for a stool to turn green or brown when left exposed to the air. If you are worried, consult your midwife or doctor, who will be able to reassure and advise you.

As a rule, loose stools are not an indication of an infection. Watery stools, however, if accompanied by a sudden change in the colour, smell, or frequency of passing, need to be mentioned to your doctor, especially if your baby is "off colour" – pale, listless, and off his food.

Blood-streaked stools are never normal. The cause may be quite minor, for instance a tiny crack in the skin around the anus, but you must still consult your doctor. Larger amounts of blood or the appearance of pus or mucus may indicate an intestinal infection, so contact your doctor immediately.

The breastfed baby By the second day, light yellow stools typical of the breastfed baby will appear. The stools are rarely hard or smelly, and may be no thicker than the consistency of cream soup.

The bottlefed baby A baby fed on formula has a tendency to have more frequent stools that are firmer, browner, and more smelly than those of a breastfed baby. They commonly tend to be rather hard. The easiest remedy for this is to give your baby a little cooled, boiled water to drink in between feeds.

What does diarrhoea mean?

Diarrhoea is a sign of irritation of the intestines and it results in loose, frequent, and watery stools. In small babies, diarrhoea always has the potential to be dangerous because of the risk of dehydration, which can develop very quickly. Contact your doctor immediately if your baby refuses food or has any of the following symptoms or signs: repeated watery stools; green and smelly stools; a fever of 38°C (100°F) or greater; pus or blood in his stools; listlessness with dark-ringed eyes. If you think your baby is dehydrated, look at his fontanelles. Depressed fontanelles are a definite sign of dehydration; in this case, contact your doctor immediately. Diarrhoea can be quickly cured if it is treated early.

You can start treating your baby yourself immediately if his diarrhoea is mild, and if he has no other symptoms or signs. Diarrhoea usually clears up well on breast milk, so continue to nurse your baby if you are breastfeeding. If mild diarrhoea doesn't improve within two days, you should check with your doctor. Drinks of mineral replacement salts formulated specially for infants may be helpful at this stage. If all goes well, you can soon return to feeding your baby as usual.

Bowel function

In the digestive process, food passes through the stomach into the small intestine and from there into the large intestine. Its waste products are stored in the rectum and then finally eliminated from the body as faeces.

Digestion All food is broken down in the body by enzymes. Digestion starts in the mouth, where the food is mixed with saliva, and continues in the stomach and the upper part of the small intestine.

Absorption Once the food has been reduced to simple molecules, it is absorbed into the bloodstream as it continues its passage through the small intestine. It then passes through the large intestine, where any water is absorbed by the body. The waste products pass on to the rectum as faeces.

Elimination Faeces are stored in the rectum and eliminated through the anus. A baby can't control, even for a second, the reflex that causes the rectum to empty. Since the gastrocolic reflex stimulates the rectum to empty every time food enters the stomach, young babies usually have a bowel movement with each feed.

Girls' nappies

A baby girl tends to wet the nappy at the centre, or towards the back if she is lying down.

✳ Some disposable day-time and night-time nappies are designed differently to take account of where a baby wets the nappy, with the padding at its thickest in the place it is needed most.

✳ You may like to buy frilly or decorative pants to cover your daughter's nappies: these look pretty under a dress for a special occasion.

About nappies

Your first choice in nappies will be between fabric and disposable types. Most parents prefer to use disposables, though an increasing consciousness of environmental issues has led many parents to reconsider the virtues of fabric nappies, which create less waste. Yet the issue is not clear cut: the detergents required to clean fabric nappies can be viewed as pollutants to the water supply, and the energy required to wash them might also be regarded as wasteful. While fabric nappies are cheaper than disposables in the long run, you need to consider the increased electricity bills for frequent washing-machine runs, and the cost in your time. What is clear is that providing that the nappy is changed as frequently as necessary, and the basic rules of hygiene are observed, your baby will be happy, whichever type of nappy you choose.

Disposable nappies

Disposable nappies make nappy changing as simple as it can be. They are easy to put on and can be discarded when they are wet or dirty. Semi and fully biodegradable nappies in a wide range of designs and styles are available now. Disposable nappies are convenient when you're travelling as you need fewer nappies and less space to change in, and you don't

Nappies and accessories

Shaped fabric nappy

Nappy liner

Elasticated leakage barriers provide extra protection

Efficient leg elastication gives a good fit so there's less chance of leaks

Absorbent inner layer has a plastic covering

Disposable nappy

have to carry wet, smelly nappies home with you to be washed. You will need a constant supply so, to avoid carrying huge loads with your shopping, buy them in large batches. Many shops will deliver nappies. Never flush disposable nappies down the lavatory as they inevitably get stuck at the S-bend. Instead, put the soiled nappy in a strong plastic bag. The bag should be firmly secured at the neck before you throw it into the bin.

Fabric nappies

Although fabric nappies are more expensive than disposables at first, they are cheaper in the long run. Fabric nappies involve more work than disposables because they have to be rinsed, washed, and dried after use, although laundry services are now available in many areas. You will need a minimum of 24 nappies to ensure that you always have enough clean ones, but the more nappies you can buy, the less often you'll have to do the washing. When buying fabric nappies, choose the best that you can afford. They'll last longer, and they'll also be more absorbent, and therefore more comfortable for your baby. Many re-usables consist of a nappy liner, an absorbent layer, and a water-resistant outer wrap.

For the absorbent layer, towelling squares can be folded in various ways (see p. 65). They are very absorbent – more so than most disposables – so they are good to use at night. Shaped terry nappies are T-shaped, made of a softer, finer towelling than squares, and have a triple-layered central panel for added absorbency. Their shape means that they are more straightforward to put on, and fit the baby more neatly.

Choose the "one-way" variety of nappy liners, which let urine pass through but remain dry next to the baby's skin, minimizing the risk of a sore bottom. Liners prevent the nappy from getting badly soiled; they can be lifted out with any faeces and flushed away.

The outer wrap, or nappy cover, prevents waste from the absorbent layer leaking out onto clothes and bedding. They are usually made of breathable, water-resistant material and fastened with poppers or Velcro.

You can also find "all-in-one" re-usable nappies on the market, which have all the features of a disposable nappy but are machine washable: they are shaped to fit, have Velcro closing tabs and elasticated legs, and are made of several layers of absorbent fabric with an anti-leak outer layer.

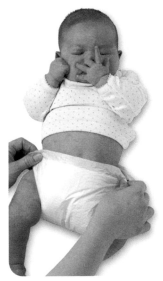

Frequent changes Young babies can't hold urine for long and it's quite normal to need to change their nappy several times a day.

Cleaning a girl

Always wipe your baby girl from front to back (towards the anus), and never clean inside the lips of the vulva.

1 Remove faeces Clean off as much faeces as possible with the front of the soiled nappy.

2 Remove urine Use a wet cloth or cotton wool to clean the genitals and surrounding skin.

3 Clean bottom Lift up her legs as shown, and wipe from front to back. Dry the area thoroughly.

Changing a nappy

Your baby's nappy will need to be changed whenever it is wet or soiled. The number of changes each day will vary from one baby to the next. As a rule though, you will probably need to change the nappy every morning when your baby wakes, before you put him to bed at night, after a bath, and after every feed. However, it's only worth changing nappies during the night if the baby has had a bowel movement.

Changing disposables is straightforward, provided you choose the nappy that is most appropriate for your baby's size so that it fits him neatly and comfortably. With fabric nappies, you can choose the type of fold that suits you and your baby, according to his age and size (see p. 65). You'll need to use liners with fabric nappies, too.

Disposable nappies

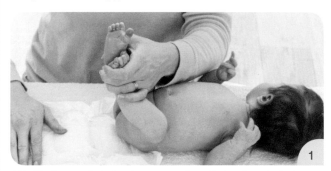

1 Positioning your baby Lay the nappy out flat, with the tabs at the back. Gently lift your baby's legs and slide the nappy under her so that the top aligns with her waist.

2 Fitting the front Take the front up between her legs and unpeel the sticky tabs at the sides.

3 Fastening the nappy Pull the tabs firmly over the front flap and press to fasten the nappy. It should fit snugly.

Folding reusable nappies

Triple absorbent fold
This is the most suitable fold for your newborn: its central panel provides good absorbency and it is very small and neat. However, it is not very suitable for larger babies. Start with a square nappy folded in four to make a smaller square, with the open edges to the top and right.

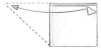

1 Pick up the top layer of the nappy by the right-hand corner.

2 Pull the corner to the left to form an inverted triangle.

3 Turn the nappy over so the point is at the top right.

4 Fold in the middle layers twice to form a thick panel.

Parallel fold This is for a larger baby. Start with a nappy laid out in a diamond shape and fold as shown.

1 Fold the top and bottom points in to overlap a bit at the centre.

2 Pick up the left-hand point and align it to the top edge; do the same with the right.

Kite fold This fold also starts with a diamond shape. You can adjust the depth of the kite to suit your baby's size.

1 Fold the sides in to the centre to form a kite shape.

2 Fold the top point down to the centre. Fold the bottom point up; vary the depth to fit.

Reusable nappies

1 Positioning the nappy Slide the nappy and liner under your baby, so that its top edge aligns with his waist. Bring the front up between his legs.

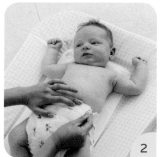

2 Fastening the nappy Fold the sides in to the centre. Hold the nappy and liner in place with one hand and do up the fastenings.

Cleaning a boy

Boys often pass urine when released from their nappy. A tissue or clean nappy laid over the penis will minimize mess.

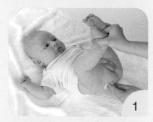

1 Remove faeces Clean off any faeces with water and cotton wool, using a fresh piece each time you wipe.

2 Remove urine Wipe with cotton wool, working from the leg creases in towards the penis. Never try to pull back the foreskin.

3 Clean bottom Lift his legs to clean his bottom by holding both ankles as shown. Dry the area well.

How to make washing easy

If you use fabric nappies, washing them will take up quite a lot of time, so use these tips to get organized and simplify your routine.

✳ Always keep a set of plastic tongs or gloves nearby. Use these to lift nappies out of the bucket.

✳ Drying nappies on radiators will make the fabric hard and uncomfortable. Use a tumble drier, an outside line, or a rack placed over the bath.

✳ You may like to use an air freshener in the nappy bucket.

Nappy hygiene

It is very important to wash nappies thoroughly; traces of ammonia will irritate your baby's skin, and faecal bacteria could cause infection. Always use non-biological detergent, since strong detergents and biological powders could also irritate your baby's skin. Fabric conditioners are not recommended for washing nappies, as they reduce the absorbency of the cloth.

Boiling nappies is not necessary unless they're very stained or have become grey; just use hot water for both rinsing and washing. If your baby's clothing gets soiled, don't add it to the nappy bucket. Remove as much of the mess as you can, rinse the garment, and wash it as usual.

Establish a washing routine

Having a washing routine will make life easier, especially if you aim to wash in large loads (to do this, you must have at least 24 nappies). You will need to store soiled nappies for long enough to make up a load. You can either do this by putting them in a dry bucket, using a drop or two of tea tree oil to minimize smells, or in a bucket half full of water, again with tea tree oil to improve the odour. (Sterilizing solutions are no longer recommended as they can damage the fittings on reusable nappies.)

Choose a bucket that is large enough to hold at least six nappies and the water (if you choose to soak), but not so large that you can't carry it when full. You can buy special nappy bins, but any good-sized bucket with a lid will do; bins designed for beer-making are ideal.

Rinse wet nappies with cold water before putting them into the bucket, to dilute the urine. With soiled nappies, remove as much faeces as possible down the lavatory and hold the nappy under the spray as you flush. Squeeze out the excess moisture and put the nappy into the bucket.

When you are ready, wash the nappies in a washing machine according to the nappy manufacturer's instructions. Dry nappies on a line if you can, as this is the cheapest way and it helps to freshen the nappies. But be careful of drying waterproof fabrics on the radiator as this can damage them. Store clean and dry nappies in the airing cupboard to ensure they are totally dry and nice and warm when you put them on your baby.

Nappy rash

If urine remains too long in a nappy or on the skin, bacteria from your baby's stools break it down to ammonia. The ammonia then irritates and burns the skin; this is the most common cause of nappy rash.

Mild nappy rash (ammonia dermatitis) will appear as small red dots and general redness around the genitals rather than the anus and you will notice a strong smell of ammonia. If it becomes more serious, you will see an inflamed area of broken skin and possibly pus-filled spots. In severe cases, it may lead to ulceration.

Breastfed babies are less prone to nappy rash than babies who are bottlefed. You'll minimize the possibility of nappy rash in any case by following the guidelines given (see right). If your baby does develop a sore bottom, check to see if it is some other rash that might need advice and treatment (see below). If not, go on with your preventive measures (except using barrier cream), as well as the following:

* Change your baby's nappy more often.
* At night (particularly If your baby sleeps through it), use a disposable pad inside a fabric nappy for extra absorbency.
* Once your baby has nappy rash, his skin needs to be aired between nappy changes for, say, 15–20 minutes.

Other rashes in the nappy area

Not all skin conditions occurring in the nappy area are true nappy rash. It's important that you identify a rash correctly so that you can take appropriate action if necessary. Use this checklist to help identify other rashes you may notice in the nappy area; some may need your doctor's advice.

* Heat rash appears as small blisters all over the nappy area in addition to a rash elsewhere on the body. If you are using plastic pants, stop. Leave your baby's nappy off whenever you have the opportunity. Cool your baby down by using fewer layers of clothes and blankets.
* Thrush appears first around the anus as a spotty rash that spreads to the buttocks and inner thighs (you may notice white patches inside your baby's mouth, too). Your doctor will probably prescribe anti-fungal treatments.
* Seborrhoeic dermatitis (very rare in babies) appears as a brownish-red scaly rash on the genitals and in skin creases, especially the groin, and anywhere the skin is greasy, such as the scalp. Your doctor will prescribe an ointment.

Preventing nappy rash

The essentials are to keep your baby's skin dry and well aired, and to make sure that nappies are always thoroughly washed and well rinsed.

* At the first sign of broken skin, start using a nappy rash cream. Creams that include titanium salts are especially effective.

* Broken skin and redness in the leg folds are caused by inadequate drying. Dry your baby meticulously and do not use talcum powder.

* Avoid washing your baby's bottom with soap, since it is likely to dry out the natural oils in his skin.

* Use disposables with a one-way lining, or one-way nappy liners with fabric nappies, to keep your baby's skin dry.

* Use a barrier cream and apply it sparingly to the affected area only (don't use this with one-way liners or disposables, however: it will clog the one-way fabric).

* Thoroughly wash and rinse nappies to make sure all traces of ammonia are removed.

* Don't leave your baby lying in a wet or soiled nappy for any longer than necessary.

* Try leaving your baby's bottom open to the air whenever you can.

Dressing up Your little girl will look lovely in a pretty dress.

First clothes

Everyone loves dressing up a baby, and your friends and family will all want to buy clothes for your baby as soon as he is born. You are bound to take great pride in his appearance and might even like to buy some dressy outfits for special occasions, but there's no need to spend a lot of money – he will grow out of his clothes very quickly. Remember that as far as your baby is concerned, anything goes as long as it's soft and comfortable to wear, and can be put on and taken off without too much disturbance.

Your baby will posset and dribble on his clothes and there are bound to be accidents and leaks from nappies, so buy only machine-washable, colour-fast clothing and avoid white: it quickly gets dirty and frequent washing makes it look drab. Look for soft, comfortable clothes with no hard seams or rough stitching. Terry cloth, cotton, or pure wool will feel nicer on your baby's skin. Synthetic fibres are soft at first but may become hard and bobbly with repeated washing.

All-in-one comfort Easy-fitting clothes will be comfortable and warm for your baby. Pay attention to the cuffs, ankles, and neck. These are the places where fastenings could chafe.

Basic wardrobe for a newborn

6 wide-necked cotton vests or T-shirts	2 loose-fitting nightdresses with drawstring ends
2 pairs socks and baby slippers	2 pairs mittens (for winter)
1 shawl for swaddling	1 padded or fleecy all-in-one outdoor suit
8 all-in-one stretch suits	
2 woollen jackets or cardigans (4 in winter)	1 hat with a wide brim and ties or elastic chin strap

Always choose clothes that are non-flammable and avoid open-weave shawls and cardigans because your baby's fingers could easily get caught in the holes of the weave. Check fastenings as well: poppers in the crotch give you easy access to the nappy, and poppers at the neck mean your baby won't grow out of a garment quickly just because his head is too big for the neck opening.

Babies hate having their faces covered, so look for wide envelope necks or clothes with front fastenings. Front-fastening clothes also allow you to dress your baby without having to turn him over. This will make the whole business of dressing more comfortable for him and easier for you.

Note your baby's measurements and take the details with you on shopping trips. Babies of the same age vary greatly in size, so read the height and weight on the label rather than the age. If in doubt, buy the larger size: loose-fitting clothes are warmer and more comfortable than clothes that are too small, and your baby will soon grow into them.

Choosing boys' clothes

Look for fabrics and designs that are practical as well as smart when choosing clothes for your baby boy.

* A dungaree and T-shirt set is very comfortable and looks smart. Look out for dungarees that have poppers at the crotch, so you have easy access to your baby's nappy while changing.

* Hats with tie-down ear-flaps are cosy in winter.

* Tights aren't just for girls. Babies lose bootees and socks easily, so tights are practical and warm, even for your little boy.

* Tracksuits are comfortable and allow easy access to the nappy.

* Strong primary colours look good on both sexes.

Day wear A smart outfit with popper fastenings is ideal for your little boy.

Nightdress Loose-fitting sleeping garments are comfortable for newborns. A drawstring at the foot end prevents the nightdress from riding up around the body and also gives you easy access to the nappy.

Keeping your baby warm

You may be anxious that your new baby is not warm enough, but a few common-sense precautions will keep him comfortable and safe. Remember that babies can easily become too hot – this could lead to heat rash and is also a factor in cot death.

✳ A great deal of body heat is lost through a bare head. Make sure your baby always wears a hat (one with a wide brim and perhaps ear-flaps as well) when you take him outdoors.

✳ Undress very young babies only in a well-heated room and out of draughts, because they cannot conserve body heat.

✳ Try to keep your baby's room at a constant temperature. The number of blankets he needs will depend on this temperature (see p. 81).

✳ If your baby is cold, you may need to warm him up. Adding a layer of clothes is not enough; put him in a warmer place first so that he can regain his normal body temperature, or hold him close to share your body heat.

✳ Never leave your baby to sleep in the sun or close to a source of direct heat, such as a radiator.

✳ Wrap your baby up if you take him outdoors, but remove his outdoor clothes when you bring him inside, otherwise he won't be able to cool down efficiently.

Dressing your baby

At first, you may feel nervous about dressing your baby and trying to support him while putting on and taking off his clothes. Dressing will become easier with practice, so just be gentle and patient until you both get the hang of it.

You need to keep both your hands free when you're dressing and undressing a young baby, so always use a flat, non-slip surface for this task – a changing mat is ideal. Your baby is very likely to cry as you take off his clothes. This is because young babies hate the feel of air on their naked bodies; they prefer to feel snug and secure. It's not because you're hurting him, so try not to get flustered by his distress.

Putting clothes on

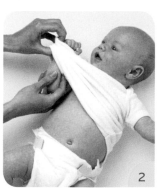

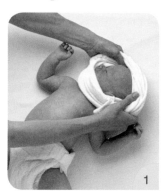

1 Putting vest over head Lay your baby on a flat, non-slip surface, and make sure his nappy is clean. Roll the vest up and widen the neck with your thumbs. Put it over the baby's head so that it doesn't touch his face, raising his head slightly as you do so.

2 Slipping arms into armholes or sleeves Widen one sleeve or armhole and gently guide your baby's arm through it. Repeat with the other arm. Pull the vest down.

3 Putting on an all-in-one suit Lay your baby on the open suit. Gather up each sleeve and guide his fists through. Open up each leg and gently guide his feet into the suit. Fasten the suit.

Taking clothes off

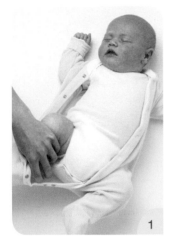

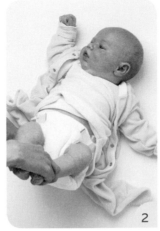

1 **Unfastening the suit** Put your baby on a flat, non-slip surface and unfasten the suit. If his nappy needs changing (see pp. 64 65), gently pull both legs out of the suit, making sure that his top half stays covered while changing.

2 **Taking off the suit** Lift up your baby's legs gently, taking care not to lift them too high, as shown in the picture. At the same time slide the suit underneath his bottom and back as far as his shoulders.

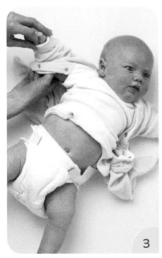

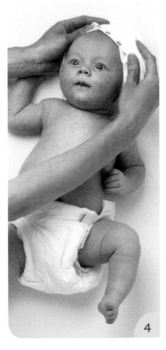

3 **Removing the top** Grasp each sleeve by the cuff and gently slide your baby's hand out of it. If he is wearing a vest, roll it up towards the neck and gently pull his arms out of its sleeves or armholes, holding him by each elbow as you do so.

4 **Taking off the vest** Spread the neck wide open with your fingers and thumbs, and lift the vest carefully over your baby's head, making sure to keep the fabric clear of his face.

Dressing on your lap

When your baby is three or four months old, he will have developed enough control of his muscles to be able to sit easily on your lap while you take off his clothes. Dealing with his bottom half may be simpler if he's lying flat.

Easy off (and on) Sit with your legs crossed so that your baby fits neatly in the hollow of your legs, and cradle him with your arm, since his back will still need some support.

More clothes

The kind of clothes you buy in addition to your baby's basic wardrobe (see p. 69) will be determined largely by your personal taste and how much money you have to spend. There is no single piece of clothing that is essential for your baby, but there are some items that are more practical than others. In summer, for instance, a cotton T-shirt and shorts or a cotton dress are the most suitable clothes because they are cool and leave the baby's limbs free; in winter, a mini pull-on track suit or dungarees worn with a neck-buttoned jumper are good alternatives to an all-in-one stretch suit. As before, stick to clothes in materials that move with your child so that there's no risk of him being uncomfortable, or of the material tearing; terry cloth, cotton, and corduroy are ideal. Make sure that his clothes provide easy access to the nappy and that they're machine washable.

Keep an eye on how tight the neck, wrists, and legs are on all clothes and buy the next size up if need be. Clothes with poppers at the neck may last longer. Babies often outgrow clothes because their heads can no longer go through the neck opening, but you can just leave poppers undone to accommodate the head. You will probably learn to gauge your baby's size quite accurately, but if you're at all worried, go by the height and weight charts given on the labels, not by age. If your child isn't with you when you're out on a shopping trip, check that the clothes can be exchanged.

As your baby gets older, you may like to dress him in a sleep suit at night as a cosy alternative to an all-in-one stretch suit. A sleeping bag will solve the problem of kicked-off blankets on very cold nights. When buying underwear, choose wide-necked vests that will easily go over your baby's head. Brightly patterned vest-and-pants sets can double up as T-shirts or pyjamas.

Chapter 5

Sleeping

Unless your newborn is hungry, cold, or uncomfortable, she'll spend **most of the time** between feeds asleep. However, don't expect your baby to sleep all the time, and don't worry if she doesn't; some babies are **naturally more wakeful** than others.

Safety measures

When planning a nursery, bear in mind that your child will be mobile before long.

✳ Make sure that the furniture' has no sharp edges or corners.

✳ Choose a non-slip floor covering and consider fitting bars and locks to the windows.

✳ Furniture should be stable so your child can't pull it over.

✳ Toys should be stored at floor level so your child doesn't have to stretch to reach them.

✳ Choose wall-mounted lamps to avoid trailing flexes.

✳ Don't overheat the nursery; overheating is a risk factor in cot death (see pp. 81–82).

The nursery

At first, your baby may have a room of her own or share yours, but once she starts sleeping through the night she should have her own space. You'll need little special equipment and you can improvise if need be with household items – a sink will do just as well as a baby bath, for instance, and a folded towel doubles up as a changing mat – but many parents do delight in the opportunity to equip a nursery.

If this is your first child, ask friends with children which items they have found most useful and then weigh up their advice against your own lifestyle. If there's anything you're unsure about, shop around and have a look through store catalogues before deciding. There will often be many things that you can manage without. The only essentials for your baby are somewhere for her to sleep, nappies, clothes (see pp. 62–63 and 68–69), and feeding equipment.

Don't feel you have to buy everything brand new; look out for second-hand items advertised in local papers or on notice boards in the local baby clinic. A carrycot will last only a couple of months because babies grow so quickly, so it makes sense to borrow one from friends or relatives if you can. If you buy second-hand items, check for general wear and tear, and make sure that all surfaces are smooth and free of rust for your baby's safety. Check, too, if they still comply with current safety regulations. Beware of painted items: many old-fashioned paints contain lead, which is toxic if ingested (your baby may suck on the side of her crib, for example). Never buy second-hand car seats or harnesses.

Basic equipment for your baby

Transport Carrycot pram (suitable from birth); pushchair or buggy; sling; infant car seat	**Sleeping** Carrycot, crib, or cot; mattress with waterproof cover; fitted cot sheets; cellular blanket (for newborn); swaddling shawls (optional); baby monitor
Bathing Baby bath (with stand); cotton wool; large soft towel; flannel or sponge; baby brush; baby bath lotion; pair of blunt-ended scissors	**Other** Bouncing chair; muslin squares

Arranging a nursery

Once you bring your baby home, you'll be too busy feeding and changing her – and probably too tired as well – to plan your nursery, so do this before she's born.

Try to ensure that the room is as easy as possible to keep clean, with wipeable surfaces. Choose furniture without hard edges or corners and make sure that all painted surfaces are non-toxic and lead-free. You'll need plenty of storage space, especially near the changing area; a wide-topped low chest of drawers with shelf space above is ideal, or you may like to build your own. Be sure the top is smooth, washable, and wide enough to accommodate the changing mat. Haircord carpet is the ideal floor covering for the nursery, since it will absorb noise and is warm and hard-wearing. If you're worried about keeping the carpet clean, vinyl or cork tiles with non-slip rugs are a good alternative.

The nursery does not have to be very warm, but it should be at a constant temperature. Around 18°C (65°F) is fine if your baby is covered with a sheet and two blankets; if the room is warmer, she should have fewer blankets (see p. 81). As long as your baby is tucked up snugly, all-night heating will be needed only in extremely cold weather. A thermostatically controlled room heater is the most suitable.

It is a good idea to fit a dimmer switch so that you can gently bring up the lights without startling your baby. You may also find a folding screen useful to protect your baby's cot from sunlight and draughts.

Visual stimulation Put an unbreakable mirror on the side of your baby's cot so that she can see her own face.

Decorating the nursery

A newborn baby has a very limited range of vision – only 20–25 centimetres (8–10 inches) – but lively colours and decorations will provide a stimulating environment.

* The cheery colours of nature are best. Pastel yellow, blue, and grassy green will soothe your baby. Enliven the room with vivid splashes of primary red, green, blue, and yellow.
* Hang mobiles above your baby's cot and the nappy changing area. Their colours and movement will make her alert to her surroundings and also help her develop the ability to focus on objects.
* Display bold, interesting pictures in bright colours on the walls and attach fluorescent stars and moons to the ceiling.
* Choose fabrics and wall coverings that are washable and have lively designs to stimulate your baby.

Your baby's bed

The best choice for your newborn baby is a Moses basket or a carrycot pram; some prams convert to pushchairs for use when she's able to support herself sitting up. Your baby will outgrow baby baskets or cradles quite quickly, so don't splash out on an expensive one unless you're sure you can afford it. When your baby outgrows her crib or carrycot, you will need a full-sized cot. Choose one with side rails set closely together – 2.5–6 centimetres (1–2½ inches) is most suitable – and with drop sides so that you can lift your baby out easily. The mattress should fit snugly, so your baby can't get her arm or her leg, or even her head, trapped down the side. The cot will last until your baby is big enough to clamber out, when you'll need to buy a bed – at about two or two-and-a-half years. The cot mattress should be new for each baby, but if not, then it should be clean, dry, firm, and flat. The outside should have a waterproof cover with no tears, cracks, or holes. Cover the mattress with a single sheet.

Travel cots are very useful for when you go on holiday or take your baby out with you for the evening. They have fabric sides and are collapsible, so they can easily be carried and stowed.

Moses basket

Places to sleep Your newborn baby will be spending much of her time asleep, and she'll be able to sleep just about anywhere. A basket or carrycot is best at first, but once she outgrows this, she'll need a cot.

Full-sized cot

As a young baby can't effectively regulate her own body temperature, you should always use a cotton sheet with cellular blankets for the cot so you can easily add a blanket or take one away. Once she is a year old, a cot duvet will be suitable. Make sure that any bedding you buy is flameproof and conforms to current safety standards.

Sleeping temperatures Research into cot death has shown that babies who get too hot are at a greater risk of cot death. While the temperature of the nursery is important, the number of blankets in your baby's cot is of greater significance. If the nursery is at 16°C (65°F), then a sheet and two layers of blankets will keep your baby at an ideal temperature. If it is warmer, you should use correspondingly fewer blankets (see p. 81).

Similarly, cot bumpers and pillows can make your baby too hot. Babies lose heat through their heads, so if your baby's head is buried in a pillow or bumper, heat loss will be reduced. These days fleeces and baby nests are not advised because the baby is at risk of overheating.

Bedtime comforts

- Clean, dry, firm, flat, waterproof-covered mattress
- Cot duvet (not for babies under 12 months)

- Cotton sheets
- Cotton cellular blanket
- Fleecy blanket

Baby monitors

A baby monitor enables you to keep in touch with your baby, even when she is in another room of the house.

* Baby monitors are available in different versions: battery, mains, or rechargeable.

* Lights indicating whether the batteries are low, or the baby unit is out of range, are useful.

Keeping in touch Monitors come in two parts – the baby's transmitter and the parents' receiver (above).

Baby's day out

Young babies sleep a lot, so you can take your baby with you anywhere and enjoy going out.

In the early weeks, it's good for mothers to get out of the house and socialize. While your baby is young, she will sleep anywhere. A car seat that doubles as a free-standing chair can be strapped in place in the car, and carried indoors. However, young babies shouldn't be left sitting upright for long periods and should be allowed to lie down.

Once your baby starts sleeping through the night, you'll need to stick to a bedtime routine, so take advantage of this flexibility while you can.

Sleeping Make sure your baby is warm and covered but not too warm (see p. 81). A picture of a face on the side of the cot will hold her attention if she's awake.

Sleep and wakefulness

A newborn baby needs a great deal of sleep and unless she is hungry, cold, or uncomfortable, it is likely that she will spend at least 60 per cent of her time asleep.

Your baby may fall asleep immediately after (and even sometimes during) a feed. She will probably pay no attention to noises such as doors shutting or the radio – in fact, she may find droning noises, such as that of a vacuum cleaner, soothing. A baby's sleeping patterns do vary, so if your baby is wakeful after a feed, don't insist that she stays in her cot.

It is important that your baby learns to distinguish day from night. When it grows dark outside, close the curtains and turn the lights very low. Make sure that she is warm and covered. When she wakes during the night, feed her quickly and quietly without turning the lights up, and don't play with her. In time, she will learn the difference between a feed during the day and one at night.

Where should your baby sleep?

It's probably easiest to let your baby sleep in something that makes her portable, such as a Moses basket. A carrycot is also suitable for both day and night, since it is easily movable and can be clipped on to a wheeled chassis when you go out. Later, though, she will need a proper cot (see p. 76).

Sleeping with you Never sleep with your baby if you or your partner are very tired, are smokers, or have been drinking or taking any drugs or medication that may cause you to sleep heavily. Sharing a bed with your baby is more risky if she was born prematurely or at a birth weight less than 2.5 kilograms (5½ pounds). Be aware of the risk that a baby sharing your bed may get caught between the wall and you, or roll out of bed, or that you or your partner may roll onto her in the night.

Your baby's bedroom You must pay careful attention to the temperature of your baby's room. Babies cannot regulate their body temperatures as well as adults, and to maintain the right level of warmth they need a constant temperature and enough blankets to keep them warm at all times – but not too warm (see p. 81). A night light or dimmer switch lets you check on your baby during the night without waking her or startling her.

Sleeping outdoors Except when it's chilly, your baby will sleep quite happily outdoors, but make sure she's wrapped up and visible at all times. Never put her in direct sunlight; either choose a shady area or protect her with a canopy. If it's windy, put the carrycot hood up so it acts as a wind-break. Be sure to put a cat net over the carrycot, too.

Clothing Your newborn's clothes will need to be changed often, and while she is sleeping she should wear something that gives you easy access to her nappy. The best garment is an all-in-one stretch suit or a nightdress with a drawstring at the foot end so it doesn't ride up her back.

It is important that your baby does not get too hot or too cold. In warm weather, a nappy and a vest will be sufficient. In winter, you can check that your baby is warm enough by touching the back of her neck with your hand. Her skin should feel about the same temperature as yours. If she feels cold, warm her by holding her close to your body. If she appears to be hot and clammy, take a blanket off and let her cool down.

Dealing with problems

If your baby wakes you frequently during the night or she cries when you try to go back to bed, you'll be short of sleep and will find it difficult to cope during the day. It is essential that you get enough rest, and you should share the responsibility of night feeds with your partner. Even if you are breastfeeding, your partner could bottlefeed your baby on some nights with your expressed milk (see pp. 42–43). Alternatively, get your partner to bring you the baby to feed and then he can change her nappy. If you're exhausted, ask a friend or relative for help, relax your routine, get up late, and take daytime naps.

Encourage your baby to sleep at night by tiring her out in the day with plenty of stimulation: talk to her, pick her up, and give her lots of different things to look at. If she wakes up very often during the night because she is wet, use double nappies or nappy liners, and if she cries when you leave her, don't return and pick her up straight away. Rocking her cot, removing a blanket, or changing her position may be sufficient to soothe her.

Early on, swaddling or wrapping your baby in a shawl or blanket may help her sleep; the sensation of being tightly enclosed gives babies a great feeling of security. It's also a useful way of calming a distressed baby. Unwrap her straight away if she feels or looks too hot.

Settling your baby down

Here are several things you can do to make sure that your baby settles down to sleep.

* In the first month or so, wrap or swaddle your baby before you put her down. However, do not keep her swaddled all night.

* To swaddle your baby, fold a shawl or small blanket into a triangle. Lay your baby on it, aligning her head with the longest edge. Fold one point of the shawl across her and tuck it firmly behind her back; do the same with the other point. Tuck the bottom of the shawl back underneath your baby's feet to keep them covered.

* Give your baby a comfort suck from your breast or a bottle.

* Darken the room at night and keep the curtains closed.

* Hang a musical mobile over the cot to soothe your baby.

* If she doesn't seem to be settling down, rock her gently or stroke her back (especially the back of her neck) or limbs to soothe her.

* Try carrying her around in a sling and jogging her up and down: your closeness and the sound of your heartbeat will help her to settle down.

By following these guidelines, you can significantly reduce your baby's risk of cot death.

* Always lay your baby to sleep on her back, and in the feet to foot position (see below).

* Do not share your bed with your baby or sleep with her on a sofa or armchair. Lay her in a cot in your room, next to your bed.

* Don't smoke or allow anyone else to do so in your house, and avoid smoky places.

* Don't let your baby get too hot.

* Cover your baby with fewer blankets if the room is warm.

* Keep your baby's head bare while she sleeps.

* Don't place pillows, duvets, or any soft materials or objects, such as stuffed toys, in the cot.

* If you think your baby is not well, contact your doctor at once.

* If your baby has a fever, don't increase the wrapping; reduce it so she can lose heat.

Feet to foot Lay your baby on her back with her feet touching the foot of the cot, even if her head is halfway down the mattress.

Preventing cot death

Sudden Infant Death Syndrome (SIDS), colloquially known as cot death, is the sudden and unexpected death of a baby for no obvious reason. The present rate for cot deaths in the UK, according to the Foundation for the Study of Infant Deaths (FSID), is less than 4 per 10,000 live births. Since the start of the Reduce the Risk campaign in 1991, the number of cot deaths has fallen by 70 per cent.

The causes of cot death are unknown, and there is therefore no advice that can guarantee its prevention. There are, however, many ways in which parents can reduce the risk of cot death. Recent surveys have proved that immunization reduces the risk, as does keeping your baby in your room with you at night for the first six months. Falling asleep with your baby on the sofa greatly increases the risk of cot death.

Sleeping position

One of the most crucial risk factors is the position in which you put your baby down to sleep. In most countries babies have traditionally slept on their backs. In the UK as well, most babies slept on their backs until the 1960s, and the number of cot deaths was low. In 1970, however, special care baby units started to lay preterm babies face down because it seemed this position improved breathing and reduced vomiting. Eventually, this practice was extended to full-term babies.

The significance of sleeping position in relation to SIDS was examined in 1965, but the evidence was not convincing. It wasn't until 1986, when SIDS rates in different communities were compared, that it became clear that SIDS was less common in babies that slept on their backs.

The safest position for your baby, therefore, is on his back. Some people will tell you that this position may allow inhalation of posset, but there is no evidence to support this.

Strong evidence against smoking

There is now no doubt that a mother who smokes during pregnancy increases the risk of SIDS. (She also increases the risk of giving birth prematurely, or having a low birthweight baby.) What's more, the risk increases in proportion to the number of cigarettes smoked. The risk of SIDS in babies born to smokers is twice that for babies born to non-smokers, and the risk increases three times with every 10 cigarettes a day.

Even more cot deaths could be avoided if all pregnant women, and mothers and fathers were to stop smoking. Studies carried out in the United States now strongly suggest that being exposed to smoke increases a baby's risk of suffering from SIDS by 200 per cent.

The importance of temperature

There's no doubt that overheating a baby by covering her with too many nightclothes and blankets, or keeping her in a room with a high room temperature, is a contributory factor, as SIDS is much more common in overheated babies. Two-thirds of cot deaths occur in winter, when babies may be wrapped up too warmly. The risk posed by overheating alone, however, is less than that from sleeping position or smoking.

Many parents increase the amount of bedding when a baby is unwell, but this is not what your baby needs. High body temperature, together with infection in babies more than 10 weeks old, greatly increases the risk of cot death. If heat loss is prevented, the body temperature of a restless baby with an infection will rise by at least 1 degree per hour. Babies lose maximum heat from their face, chest, and abdomen, so lying on the back allows better control of body temperature.

Baby nests, sheepskins, duvets, and cot bumpers are all heat insulators, and so should not be used for young babies, because they prevent heat loss. There is no need to heat the nursery all night unless the weather is very cold; just make sure that your baby has enough blankets (see chart below). If you do have a heater in her room, use a thermostatically controlled one that will switch off if the room gets too warm and switch back on again when it cools down.

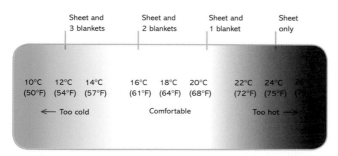

Sheet and 3 blankets			Sheet and 2 blankets			Sheet and 1 blanket		Sheet only
10°C (50°F)	12°C (54°F)	14°C (57°F)	16°C (61°F)	18°C (64°F)	20°C (68°F)	22°C (72°F)	24°C (75°F)	
← Too cold			Comfortable				Too hot →	

Controlling the temperature Keep a thermometer in your baby's room so that you can see how many blankets she needs (see chart). These guidelines are for babies wearing a nappy, vest, and sleep suit.

Coping with cot death

The unexpected death of an infant is bereavement of a particularly painful kind, but support is available to help parents cope with their feelings of bewilderment, grief, and guilt (see Useful Addresses, p. 93).

* Many parents seek help straight after the death. Telephone support lines are available that can offer you information and a sympathetic listener.

* In the longer term, parents may seek professional help. The continued support of a health visitor, social worker, or religious adviser can be invaluable, so don't be afraid to ask.

* Parents may be helped by being able to talk to someone who has gone through the same experience, either in support groups or on a one-to-one basis.

* Some areas have befriending schemes that continue long after professional help may have ceased, and these can be invaluable at times of particular grief, such as the baby's birth and death anniversaries.

* Parents who have lost one baby through cot death are likely to be extremely anxious when another baby is born. Support schemes exist that involve the parents, midwife, doctor, and health visitor in making sure the new baby gets the best possible care.

Continuing research

Although risk factors have been identified, the causes of cot death are still not close to being understood. Ongoing areas of research include the development of a baby's temperature control mechanisms and respiratory system in the first six months of life, and the discovery that an inherited enzyme deficiency may be responsible for a small number (around 1 per cent) of cot deaths.

A recent study in the UK connected cot death with flame-retardant chemicals in cot mattresses, but the connection has not been definitely proven yet.

Chapter 6

Going out and about

Your new baby **can go everywhere** with you as long as you are prepared. If you are **organized and confident,** outings with your baby can be a joy, and the sooner you **start getting out and about** the better.

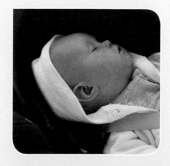

Walking and carrying

Your baby will spend most of his time being carried, wheeled, or secured in some way, and there is a wide variety of prams and carriers available for this. Safety and portability should be your main considerations when choosing this equipment.

A sling is by far the most popular way of transporting a newborn: it's light and comfortable, and allows you to carry your baby close while keeping both hands free. Try one on with your baby inside before you buy it, and make sure that it supports his head comfortably. A backpack is suitable once your baby can sit up by himself. These usually have a supportive frame that makes bearing a larger baby's weight easier.

For longer journeys, you will need a pram or pushchair in which your baby can sit or lie down. For the first three months, or until he has head control, you should use one in which he can lie flat. The pram you choose will depend on your budget and lifestyle. Consider where you will keep it and whether you will need to take it on buses and trains, or up and down a staircase. Whatever pram you choose, it should have a built-in harness, or rings to fix one in place.

A hood shield will protect your baby from rain

Make sure that the brakes are easy to use

The top lifts off and can be used as a carrycot

Choosing a pram For the first three months your baby must be able to lie flat. Reclining pushchairs are available, but a carrycot pram is more versatile and can be used for longer. Some models can be converted to pushchairs.

Carrying your baby

Using a sling Your baby will feel safe and secure inside a sling. It will also leave your arms free. The sling should have a support to hold your baby's head comfortably.

Using a backpack This is the ideal transport once your baby gets too heavy for a sling. Make sure that he is comfortable and that the leg openings don't restrict him.

Using a bouncing chair When you're out visiting friends with your baby, you can take along a bouncing chair. Your baby can be propped up in the chair so that he can look and see what is happening around him. Always put the chair on the floor, and never on a table or worktop.

Safety harnesses

Your young baby has no fear of falling, so wherever he sits he will have to be strapped in for his own safety.

* A five-point harness, which has straps for the shoulders as well as the waist and crotch, is the safest kind.

* Your baby's pram should have either a built-in harness, or fixing points so that you can attach one on your own.

* High chairs often have a built-in crotch strap. They should also have rings to take a safety harness, which can be bought separately.

* Many harnesses come with optional reins that you can attach when your baby is old enough to walk.

Travel and outings

Time spent planning a trip or regular travel is never wasted. The younger your baby, the more you will have to plan. In the first few months, your baby's feeding schedule may not be very predictable, so you'll need all ingredients to make up at least one bottle of feed if you're not breastfeeding, as well as your usual changing equipment (lightweight bags with portable changing mats are widely available). Plan your route so that you know where you can stop and where you can change and feed your baby without embarrassment or inconvenience. If you are planning to shop it is worth ringing up stores to find out if they have a mother-and-baby changing room, and avoiding those that don't have this convenience.

If your baby is just a few weeks old, it's simply not worth undertaking a busy outing where you will have to walk a great deal, carry heavy loads, or make lots of changes of transport. Be easy on yourself. Take a friend or your partner with you if you can so there is always an extra pair of hands and someone to help you should you get into a scrape. Your baby can go anywhere with you as long as you are well prepared and have something in which to carry him – a sling, pram, or car seat.

Using a pushchair

If you do not want to carry your baby in a sling, a pushchair is ideal for a small baby, who will fit comfortably and snugly into it. Babies take an interest in their surroundings from a very early age, so as soon as your baby can sit up angle the pushchair so that he can see what is going on around him.

You must become adept at collapsing and opening the pushchair within a few seconds without any problems, so practise at home before your first outing. If you can't fold up the pushchair efficiently, you will find people jostling to get in front of you when you are in a queue, which will just add to your frustration. At the very least, you should be able to open the pushchair with only one hand, kick it shut with your feet, and know how to operate the brakes – and don't forget that you will have to do all these things while holding your baby. Here are a few safety tips:

✳ When you open your pushchair, always make sure that it is in the fully extended position with the brakes fully locked.

✳ Never have your baby in the pushchair without firmly securing him in place with the safety harness.

* Never ever leave your baby in a pushchair unattended.
* Should your baby fall asleep in the pushchair, adjust it to the lie-back position so that he can sleep comfortably.
* Don't put shopping on the pushchair handles – it can unbalance the pushchair and your baby may be injured.
* When you stop, always put the brakes on because you could inadvertently take your hands off the pushchair and it might roll away.
* Check your pushchair regularly to make sure the brakes and catches work properly and that the wheels are solid.

Public transport

Using public transport can be a real trial, since neither buses nor trains are usually equipped for mothers and young children. Picture yourself with a pushchair, a heavy, wriggling baby, the baby-changing bag, your handbag, a coat, and possibly a toddler in tow, and public transport becomes the last thing you want to face.

Of course, you can make life easier by never travelling in the rush hour or, with a young baby, carrying him around in a sling. For an older baby, a backpack makes you much more independent, since having your hands free means you can manage everything more easily. Always prepare yourself well ahead of time. I simply would not leave home with my children without carrying some distracting toys, an interesting book, and a favourite snack.

All your belongings, including the pushchair, should be collected together prior to leaving and in good enough time so that you can check them over to make sure nothing is forgotten. The same goes for when you are getting off a bus or train: be ready in plenty of time for your stop. Always ask fellow passengers for help.

Special outings

Looking after your baby doesn't mean that you can't resume the active and enjoyable life you had before. Dinner in a favourite restaurant or a trip to the cinema will make a welcome diversion in your busy and demanding new routine (but avoid smoky places). Your baby is never too young for an outing, either – with a young baby you can go just about anywhere and, provided he can look about him, he will enjoy and be stimulated mentally as well as visually by the change of scene, even if he understands little of what's going on.

Managing with two children

An outing with just one baby can be a challenge if you are not confident. With a toddler in tow as well you will need to be especially organized.

* A double pushchair with sections that are independently adjustable is ideal for children of different ages.

* Carry your newborn in a sling, leaving your hands free for your toddler's pushchair.

* Four hands are better than two: any trip will be easier with your partner or a friend.

* Take a snack, such as fresh fruit, a drink of diluted fruit juice, and a favourite book, toy, or comforter for your toddler.

* Attach toys to the pushchair so you don't have to pick them up again and again.

* Avoid having to use public transport or escalators.

* Postpone a special outing that you've planned if your toddler is in a bad mood that day, or if you no longer feel like making the trip.

Shopping with your baby

Whenever you take your baby shopping with you, always plan all your movements and stops in detail so that you can use your time most efficiently.

* Try to fit in a shopping trip between feeds. If you are bottlefeeding and you think the trip is going to be longer than the usual interval between meals, take ingredients for preparing a bottle of feed with you (see p. 49).

* Always take basic changing equipment in case your child needs a clean nappy. Most big stores have mother-and-baby changing facilities.

Harness and reins Keep your baby safe in her pushchair by firmly securing her with the harness. You'll be able to use the reins and anchor straps when she's older.

Shopping trips and car journeys

Taking a young baby shopping has its own problems. Even if you are going to be out for only an hour or two, he can easily get bored, hungry, fretful, and difficult to manage, so it's worth planning ahead quite carefully to minimize stress. Taking a car will make a world of difference: you can feed and change your baby in it, you can load your shopping in the boot and not have to carry cumbersome bags, and you won't have to worry about using public transport.

If you don't own a car, you might want to borrow a relative's car. If you don't drive, it may be worth asking a friend who does to join your shopping expedition. Try to shop fairly early in the day when the streets and shops are less busy and there are fewer distractions for your baby. Always try to give your baby a good meal before you leave; that way, you may have two or three hours to complete all your purchases without him getting hungry or distressed.

Take whatever equipment you would have with you on any other trip, including feeding and changing equipment. Toys may seem something of a burden, but they will more than pay their way, since you can attach them to the backpack, pushchair, or supermarket trolley for your child to play with, and not have to keep on picking them up.

Carrying your baby

You need to have your hands free for shopping, and so how you carry your baby is worth some thought and attention. Once your baby is able to sit up with good head and back control, you can put him into your shopping trolley. Many supermarkets now have trolleys with integral baby seats and harnesses, but with the older, tip-up kind of seat you need to strap your baby in with a harness. A backpack is ideal for carrying your baby on shopping trips: his interest will be continuously engaged, he'll feel secure with such close physical contact, he should be well-behaved and cry very little, and your hands will be free. Since babies are always grasping and reaching for interesting objects, walk down the centre of the supermarket aisles so that he isn't tempted to dislodge tins and packets. Best of all, ask your partner to go shopping with you and get him to carry the baby on his back so that you are free to select and make the purchases.

Longer journeys by car

Your baby is bound to become fretful in the cramped circumstances of a long journey. It's your job to make sure that he is cool, fed, changed without fuss, and has enough to distract him when he's not sleeping. If the weather is hot, he will become fretful more easily than if it is warm or cool. Never leave your baby alone in a car in hot weather: the temperature can get much higher inside the car than outside, causing him to get quickly overheated and even dehydrated. Always screen your child from bright sunlight by putting a custom-made blind over the window through which the sun is shining, or attach a canopy to your baby's seat, which will serve the same purpose.

Car safety

Above all, you need to transport your baby safely in a car. By law, your child must be safely restrained in a car, so make sure you have a suitable safety seat fitted even before you take your baby home from the hospital. All children should travel in a child seat that is suitable for their weight and size. A young baby should go in a rear-facing car seat, but never use a rear-facing car seat in the front seat of a car fitted with airbags. Never sit in the front with an unrestrained baby, because if the car stops suddenly your baby will be flung out of your arms and will certainly be injured. An older baby should sit in a front-facing car seat.

After any accident, replace your seat belts, your child's car seat, and the anchorage kit, as they will have been badly strained and may be damaged. For the same reason, never buy secondhand car seats, harnesses, or anchorage kits.

Feeding and changing

Breastfeeding really comes into its own on a journey, but never feed your baby when the car is moving because it is not safe to do so. If you are bottlefeeding, make sure you have all the ingredients you require to prepare a bottle of formula on the move (see p. 49). Never try to keep made-up feeds warm, as you will only be letting germs multiply.

Take disposable nappies, even if you normally use fabric ones. You can always change your baby on the back seat of the car, on a rug, or on a towel in the boot. You only need to top and tail him, but be meticulous about cleaning the nappy area. Always take baby wipes, a sealable container or plastic bags for dirty nappies, and nappy cream to prevent nappy rash.

Length and weight

Boys' length and weight 0–6 months

When you assess your baby's progress, the most important criteria are his happiness and general well-being. However, you may find it interesting to plot your baby's increasing length and weight on these charts (see right).

Don't become anxious unless your baby's growth pattern veers away from the centile line (see below). Try not to compare your child to others of his age.

The range of "normal" heights or weights at any given age can vary. A newborn boy may weigh between 2.5 and 4.5 kilograms (5½–10 pounds) without giving cause for concern.

Each chart shows the range of lengths or weights into which the majority of children will fall. The dotted line in the middle of each graph represents the 50th centile, that is, 50 per cent children will fall below the line and 50 per cent above it. The outer lines stand for extremes beyond which very few children (less than 0.5 per cent) will fall, but if your child does, consult your doctor.

A child's measurements, plotted regularly, should form a line that is roughly parallel to the central line. If not, the measurements may be incorrect or the wrong chart may have been used. Consult your local clinic if you feel in any doubt about your baby's progress.

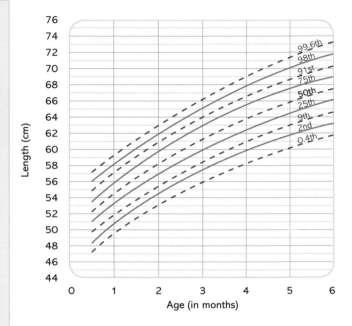

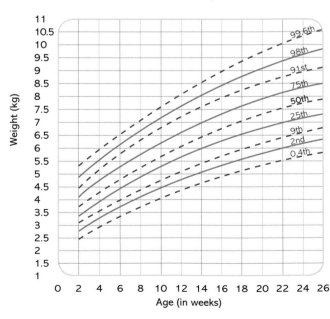

Girls' length and weight 0–6 months

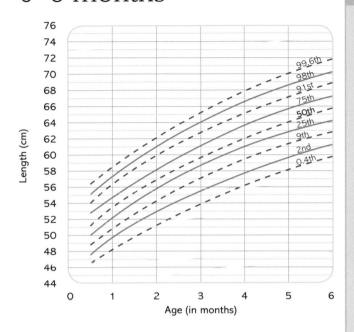

Using the charts

I believe that no baby needs to be measured and weighed if he's obviously thriving, but we've included these charts for parents who are keen to follow their child's progress.

✳ You will probably need to ask your midwife or hospital doctor for your baby's birthweight and birth length.

✳ Chart your baby's progress using the measurements taken by your doctor or health visitor, or from readings done at your local baby clinic.

✳ Special charts are available for babies with low birthweights. You can ask your health visitor for more details.

✳ To keep track of your baby's progress with the charts, find his age along the bottom axis and draw a straight line up from it. Now find his length or weight along the vertical axis and draw a line across. Mark a solid dot where the two lines meet. With each week, you'll be able to enter another dot. The emerging row of dots is your baby's growth curve.

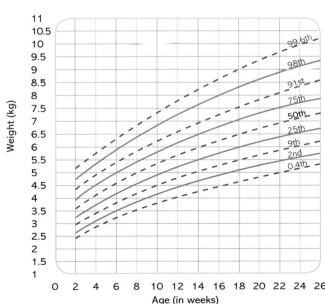

Chart data sources:
UK1990 reference data, reanalysed 2009, and WHO Child Growth Standards (WHO Multicentre Growth Reference Study Group)

Your baby's first milestones

Use this space to record your baby's earliest milestones, for instance, his first smile.

....
....
....
....
....
....
....
....
....
....
....
....
....
....
....
....
....
....
....
....
....
....
....
....
....

Baby records

You may think that the exact details of your baby's birth are unforgettable, but you'll find that your memory becomes hazy with time. These birth records, and the length and weight charts, will jog your memory and help you keep track of your baby's progress in his first six months of life.

First baby
Name..
Estimated date of delivery...
Date and time of birth...
Place..
Length...
Weight...
Blood group..
Duration of labour..
Type of delivery..
Midwife/consultant...
People present..

Second baby
Name..
Estimated date of delivery...
Date and time of birth...
Place..
Length...
Weight...
Blood group..
Duration of labour..
Type of delivery..
Midwife/consultant...
People present..

Useful addresses

Postnatal support

Association of Breastfeeding Mothers
PO Box 207, Bridgwater,
Somerset, TA6 7YT
Tel: 0870 401 7711
www.abm.me.uk
Email: info@abm.me.uk

Association for Postnatal Illness
145 Dawes Road,
London SW6 7EB
www.apni.org
Email: info@apni.org

La Leche League
129a Middleton Boulevard,
Wollaton Park,
Nottingham, NG8 1FW
Tel: 0845 456 1844
www.laleche.org.uk
Email: enquiries@laleche.org.uk

MAMA (Meet-a-Mum Association)
54 Lillington Road
Radstock, BA3 3NR
Tel: 0845 120 3746
www.mama.co.uk
For isolated or depressed mothers

NCT
Alexandra House,
Oldham Terrace
Acton, London W3 6NH
Tel: 0870 770 3236
www.nctpregnancyandbabycare.com
Email: enquiries@national-childbirth-trust.co.uk

NHS National Breastfeeding Helpline
Helpline: 0300 100 0212
www.nationalbreastfeedinghelpline.org.uk

Recruitment and Employment
Confederation
Albion House, Chertsey Road
Working
Surrey, GU21 6BT
Tel: 020 7009 2100
www.rec.uk
Email: info@rec.uk.com

The Breastfeeding Network
PO Box 11126, Paisley
PA2 8YB
Tel: (supporterline): 0300 100 0210
www.breastfeedingnetwork.org.uk

Parents' groups

BLISS (Baby Life Support Systems)
68 South Lambeth Road
London SW8 1RL
Tel: 0500 618140
www.bliss.org.uk

For parents of special care babies

CRY-SIS Support Group
BM Cry-Sis,
London WC1N 3XX
Tel: 0845 122 8669
www.cry-sis.org.uk
Email: info@cry-sis.org.uk
Advice on babies who cry excessively

Foundation for the Study of
Infant Deaths
Artillery House
11–19 Artillery Row
London SW1P 1RT
Tel: 020 7233 2090
www.sids.org.uk/fsid
Available 24 hours

Multiple Births Foundation
Hammersmith House – Level 4
Queen Charlotte and Chelsea Hospital
Du Cane Road, London W12 0HS
Tel: 020 8383 3519
www.multiplebirths.org.uk
Email info@multiplebirths.org.uk

National Council for One-Parent
Families
255 Kentish Town Road
London NW5 2LX
Tel: 0800 018 5026
www.oneparentfamilies.org.uk
Email: info@oneparentfamilies.org

Parentline Plus
520 Highgate Studios
53–79 Highgate Road
London NW5 1TL
Tel: 0808 800 2222
www.parentlineplus.org.uk
Helpline for all ages

First aid and safety

British Red Cross
UK Office, 44 Moorfields
London EC2Y 9AA
Tel: 0870 170 7000
www.redcross.org.uk

Child Accident Prevention Trust
4th Floor, Cloister Court
22–26 Farringdon Lane
London EC1R 3AJ
Tel: 020 7608 3828
www.capt.org.uk
Email: safe@capt.org.uk

Royal Society for the Prevention
of Accidents (RoSPA)
Edgbaston Park
353 Bristol Road
Birmingham B5 7ST
Tel: 0121 248 2000
www.rospa.com
Email: help@rospa.com

St. Andrew's Ambulance Association
St. Andrew's House
48 Milton Street, Cowcaddans
Glasgow G4 0HR
Tel: 0141 332 4031
www.firstaid.org.uk

Children with special needs

Association for Spina Bifida and
Hydrocephalus (ASBAH)
Asbah House, 42 Park Road
Peterborough
PE1 2UQ
Tel: 01733 555988
www.asbah.org
Email: into@asbah.org

Contact-a-Family
209–211 City Road
London EC1V 1JN
Helpline: 0808 808 3555
www.cafamily.org.uk
Email: info@cafamily.org.uk

Cystic Fibrosis Trust
Alexandra House
11 London Road
Bromley
Kent BR1 1BY
Tel: 020 8464 7211
www.cftrust.org.uk

Down's Syndrome Association
Langdon Down Centre
2a Langdon Park
Teddington TW11 9PS
Tel: 0845 230 0372
Email: info@downs-syndrome.org.uk

Index

Acknowledgments

Dorling Kindersley would like to thank the following individuals and organizations for their contribution to this book.

Jacket Image: Front
DK Library: Ruth Jenkinson

Photography
Ruth Jenkinson: pages 6, 7, 36, 37, 38, 39, 40, 41, 46, 48, 49 (column), 68, 76 (top), 80, 84, 85

All other photographs by Jules Selmes. The publisher would like to thank the following for their kind permission to reproduce their photographs:
Alamy Images: Sally and Richard Greenhill page 57; **Science Photo Library**: Ron Sutherland page 13 bottom;
Corbis Tetra Images page 88;
Getty Images Tony Anderson page 77

Illustration: Aziz Khan

DK would like to thank Lizzie Ette (health visitor) and Dr Vivien Armstrong for medical advice, and Angela Baynham for proofreading.

All other images © Dorling Kindersley
For further information see:
www.dkimages.com